Passive Income

An Ultimate Guide from Beginner to Expert, New Ideas to Gain Financial Freedom 2019

BY | Les Park

Table of Contents

Introduction

"Passive income" has gained a reputation as some sort of fairy tale. A stream of money that continues flowing even if you stop working? Must be too great to be true. In fact, it's feasible, at least in a few ways- and this book will probably tell you how you can create it for yourself.

We'll start by debunking the myths surrounding this concept, then address what it IS and how YOU can achieve it realistically. After that we'll explore the advantages of online business and just why there's no better time than now to get into business for yourself. Next, we'll explore ten methods to build an income online. We'll cover ways to profit from working with the world's largest on the web retailer by designing shirts, publishing your own book, creating your own shop, or promoting products to your audience simply. And you'll also learn to monetize your online existence with a blog, your own Shopify store, or actually an online course.

The internet is filled up with opportunities to make money, and there is absolutely no limit to how much you can generate! This guide also contains pointers on how to maintain yourself in the right mindset for achievement and build healthy practices to reach your targets. When you're carried out, you'll be ready to start out building your personal online success!

There are many books on this subject out there, so thanks again for choosing that one! Every effort was made to make certain that it's full of as much useful details as possible. Please enjoy!

Let Know:

THE REALITY about Passive Income

The concept of making money when you sleep has drawn a crowd to the pursuit of passive income. Theoretically, you put in some time and money in the start, then relax and let the money pour in when you focus on other things. This appears like a dream become a reality, but it's mostly only a dream.

By definition, passive income does mean that you don't need to be present to make money directly, but it still requires effort initially and at least some maintenance afterwards. The truth of creating passive income is even more involved than a lot of people think, but it may be worth it still.

In today's workforce, relying on one income source is risky. Job protection is rarely guaranteed, and a little extra cash is useful always. By using your primary income source to cover basic expenses, you may use extra income streams to pay off debts, reduce your economic burden, or avoid going further into debt when you are able to pay for larger purchases up front rather than with a credit card or loan.

Beyond being a great way to make extra cash on the side, creating multiple income streams is a smart way to keep your finances more secure. If you lose one work or choose to go a different path, you'll still have various other sources of income to help you through the transition.

Active income is received through direct involvement and energetic maintenance of an income stream. When the energetic involvement stops, the income stream stops flowing. The simplest exemplory case of active income is operating a traditional job. You invest period and attention and in exchange, a wage is received by you. If you don't show up to function or you obtain fired, you no longer receive wages.

Conversely, passive income is cash that continues to pay out following the initial work is done. Traditionally, income that were considered "passive" generally included money earned from investments in shares or profit acquired by a person who had invested in accommodations property but wasn't involved in the management or day-to-day functions of that property.
These are great ways to make passive income still, although they require a substantial investment right from the start. With the rise of the internet, the potential to develop passive income is around every corner if you know where to look, and you will get started with much smaller investments.

Passive income isn't a "get rich quick" scheme. Creating passive income requires "front loading," or investing lots of time or money up front. It may take period to see amazing outcomes, which explains why it in fact does take continued function and maintenance on the part of the individual. To be able to actually draw customers to your website, you'll have to continually find ways to market your business and, eventually level it up in order that it will require less energetic maintenance on your part.

Although you absolutely can drastically reduce the amount of time you may spend working throughout the full week, a passive income stream won't be quite passive fully. In order to ensure you possess a well-curved understanding of all aspects of your business, it is suggested to be as included as you can be in the start. You can then outsource whatever you don't want to do or that you aren't well-suited for to experts, or automate with software.

Among the great perks of working online is that you can have got multiple businesses creating income for you without the trouble of owning or renting different buildings, hiring managers, personnel, maintenance, etc.; or trying to find and attract a person base in your area. Your online businesses could be available to anyone across the globe twenty-four hours a time, 3 hundred sixty-five days a full year. With outsourcing and automation, these tools can grow your client base and make you money any moment of day or night with minimal involvement on your own part.

It's never too late to begin with building passive income, and you don't need to be a trained businessperson to begin with building your own business online. If you are ready to put in your time and effort to learn and improve as you move, you can build an effective business and passive income stream in addition to anyone. With an online business, you will be your own boss and work from you want anywhere. And the best part is that there is no cap on how much money you may make. With patience and persistence, you can perform the financial freedom we all fantasy of, and you can eventually reduce your functioning hours to less than those of a part-time job while still maintaining plenty of income.

Why would YOU?

The Advantages of Online Businesses

Since the World Wide Web was invented in 1990, it has grown into a network so pervasive that it's imbedded into nearly every facet of our personal and professional lives. It offers revolutionized many industries and progressed our culture significantly.

Of the adult American population, a 77% most individuals own a smartphone, and an 89% majority accesses the internet frequently. In adults between 18 to 29 years old, the percent of internet surfers sits at 98%, and for those between 30 and 49 years, it sits at 97%.

People are utilising the web more often and for more tasks than ever before, and with this development comes the opportunity to profit. Customers want to gain access to services and products from the comfort of their own homes, and someone gets to be the main one providing those goods and services.

The first secure purchase made on the internet occurred in 1994, and by 2017, online retail sales raked in USD $2.3 trillion for 10.2% of worldwide retail sales. The money being spent on the internet is continuing to grow immensely in a few brief decades, and it shows no sign of stopping.

In recent years, unemployment and underemployment rates have already been high, and the most reliable fields can't offer job security even. By going into business for yourself, you no longer place the control of your employment in the hands of another person. More and more specialists are turning toward self-employment and entrepreneurship to become free financially, create a secure existence for themselves, and be in charge of their own careers.

Becoming your own boss lets you work when you wish, where you need, and how you need with no limit to how much cash you can earn. Creating multiple streams of passive income leaves you with the assurance wherein even if one stream reduced or disappeared, you'd still be okay.

Creating an online business is the perfect method to start out your entrepreneurial journey. Whether you're just searching for a part hustle to create some extra cash or trying to make a dependable income of over seven numbers as your very own boss, the internet is definitely a hotbed of chance of money making. It's easier than ever before to get started, with the potential to possess little to no startup costs included.

Services are available to automate or outsource just about any aspect of your business, thus it's possible to run a totally hands-off operation while still raking in the dough- and the potential is limitless.

When you work for another person, your income is limited to the amount of hours you work or the worthiness someone else has attached to your services and experience. When you build yourself an internet business, your only limit is yourself. With the proper entrepreneurial mindset, a willingness to continue learning and growing, and the perseverance to power on, you can earn additional money than you even dreamed realistically possible.

In the old days, if you wanted to get into business for yourself, you'd to find a service or product that people in your area want to buy; rent or purchase a building to perform your store out of; hire administration, workers and staff to run your company; purchase utilities and janitorial costs to maintain your store or offices; and make sure that someone was open to open and close your business every full day. Then you had to discover and attract customers who wanted your service or product and pay for advertising to attract foot-visitors to your store. Even if you could actually outsource every part of the business to other people, the expenses for owning a physical business would be pretty high.

The beauty of the web is that most of these continuing business requirements disappear completely. You no longer require to pay for a full roster of part-period or full-time employees when the work you should be done only requires the casual contracted freelancer. Running a digital business eliminates the expenses associated with having a physical business area, and the products or services you can provide aren't dictated by the neighborhood market.

Thanks to the web, our location no longer plays a substantial role in our ability to interact with people. You can speak with someone on the entire opposite side of the globe as easily as you can communicate with a neighbor across the street. Your business may also benefit from this connectivity. Your customer bottom is no longer limited by geography or the number of clients you can draw to your physical shop, and your employees don't have to travel to your place of work. An online business anywhere is available, anytime of day or night time, on any full time of the year. Your customer foundation can span the entire globe, which gives you unlimited prospect of business growth virtually. And thanks to currency conversion software, it's much easier to accomplish business globally.

Your visitors aren't the only ones who can benefit from your business's global capability. As your own boss, you can travel anywhere you wish without having to use up your limited vacation times or ask for time off work. Most of us dream of getting the freedom to visit whenever and wherever we want, and running an online business is the perfect method to build your life as an electronic nomad. As long as a computer is had by you and an web connection, you can keep track of your business, access your information, talk to your employees, and earn money from you please anywhere. Because your business will run nearly entirely digitally, almost every aspect of the work could be outsourced on digital platforms to freelancers or regular workers. This is more environmentally friendly since it gives you and your employees to commute much less. It saves on time, gasoline bills, and transportation expenses, as well as significantly reduces gas emissions by reducing the real number of automobiles on the roads. Digital communications and record keeping also cuts down on paper waste and enables you to very easily gather and shop more information in a more accessible fashion.

More and more businesses are showing up online, which not only creates stiffer competition in the web marketplaces but also illustrates the high demand for online products and services. Within an offline business such as a physical store, it will be very much harder to keep an eye on other businesses in your market and figure out how to make yours much better than the competition. In the online world, it's easier to discover and evaluate your competition, as well as match their business. You can also monitor and evaluate your own company's successes and failures in product sales and advertising, making it much easier for you to figure out what's operating and what isn't, and you'll be able to better invest your time and effort and money into beneficial business decisions. Your customer service can also be improved since it is simpler for customers to get hold of you via email or your website and leave you responses so you can better focus on your target consumers.

The internet creates many benefits for your business itself clearly, but this arrangement benefits your individual life as well also. Being your own boss offers you the independence to structure your life the way you wish and the fulfillment of seeing the direct results of your time and efforts. Working for yourself does still require period and effort- but you get to decide when, where, and how you work. In the event that you do your greatest work at night, schedule your work hours for that point. If you like to settle until 10 a.m., go for it. You could work your business around your personal life rather than vice versa, and therefore have significantly more time to invest in your loved ones and personal relationships. You can put on what you would like rather than needing to follow a professional dress code, and you will even work from your own bed or couch in your pajamas in the event that you feel like it.

Your focus could be on building your business rather than all the distracting areas of working for another person, and the amount of stress you deal with can decrease. It can still be very stressful to be an online entrepreneur, but when you're focusing on something you're passionate about and viewing the beneficial rewards of your time and efforts, the stress is a lot more worthwhile.

By doing even more fulfilling work and having the freedom to build the entire life you desire, being self-employed is already an intensify from working at the decision of a big company. Having an online business brings it a step forward by enabling you to take up a business with a smaller financial purchase, lower maintenance expenses, and fewer restrictions on your business growth and income. It gets better still when you add-in the fact that on the web businesses can be outsourced and automated so thoroughly that you could keep getting paid without any direct involvement. The web never sleeps, so your business could be running 24/7 and you can rake in passive income, whilst you sleep in until 10 o'clock.

WAY 1: Affiliate Marketing

Affiliate marketing is among the most popular ways to produce passive income online. And it doesn't always require any financial expense, though it can be helpful to invest in building your website, in article marketing, and advertising. Selling services or products as an affiliate marketer involves promoting them and finding a flat rate commission or percentage of income from each sale created from your link. Essentially, the company offers you a personalized link that you tell your audience, whether it be on a blog, a contact list, a site, or an web store. When readers or viewers click through your hyperlink and make an obtain the ongoing company you're working with, you get paid.

It's generally best to let your visitors know that you're an affiliate marketer and may profit from their purchase, so it's important to build a relationship with your viewers where they trust your opinion when you vouch for a brand. If your target audience thinks you're selling them products so you can profit just, they'll be less likely to buy through your link. Aiming to help customers better their lives will constantly sell better than pushing something at them.

You can incorporate internet affiliate marketing into your already-established online presence. Links can be shared in your site posts, on your website, or through your email list using different methods to attract clients toward the products you're recommending. In the event that you don't already have a blog page or website, it's smart to begin one if you want to pursue affiliate marketing to obtain passive income. You can create a Shopify store also. Whatever avenue you choose to make use of in posting your links, you'll have to build a status or brand in a particular niche in order to become a credible expert in your niche.

In order to select a niche, make a list of topics you're already educated or passionate about and cross-reference that with a list of profitable niches. An excellent niche is one that has a popular for products and is not overly saturated with online marketers already. You need area to grow your business.

However, you do wish at least some competition in your niche and that means you know that it is already profitable more than enough to draw additional online business owners. You'll also wish to look for a niche which has a large amount of product vendors so the selection of products you can share is larger, rather than all of the affiliates will be marketing the same items. Ensure there is a demand for the merchandise in your market by checking Best Sellers lists on Amazon and additional retailers more specific to your niche.

Before you select an affiliate network, you'll have to have a real way to talk about your links with your audience. To build your website, you'll require a domain. If you don't curently have a name for your brand or store, choose your name predicated on what domain can be available, purchase your domain, buy and setup hosting then. Your domain is like your actual business, and the hosting is like the virtual real estate where your business lives.

Once you have your domain and hosting secured, install WordPress and choose a theme. There are plenty of free themes to select from and they're all very customizable. You can create your own site without any coding knowledge, or you can outsource this step to a freelancer if you would like to end up being sure your site looks nice. It should be basic, clean looking, and easy to get around. You don't want your readers to become bombarded with ads, crazy colors, or an overwhelmingly cluttered site.

Also be sure your website includes a professional logo together with your business's or brand's name onto it, and that it's mobile friendly. This site will be used to share your affiliate links, but in order to build trust and credibility together with your audience, you'll also have to offer something more.

Informative posts about studies and trends which come up in your niche can help drive traffic to your website and build your audience, but you don't need to take up a blog necessarily. Your site can host guest bloggers or content material creators in your market so that your target audience has one central spot to find the various content they're thinking about. Videos and blog posts are most likely to get organic traffic by showing up in searches.

The important thing to keep in mind is that your visitors have to trust and respect that the suggestions coming from your site will be the reliable suggestions of an authority in your niche. You may also create a product page on your own site where you feature your affiliate marketer products with links to buy them.
Blogging and creating your very own content is one of the best methods to build the reputation and credibility you should be a successful affiliate marketer. Producing high-quality content frequently allows your viewers and readers to be accustomed to your content, grow a relationship with your blog page, and continue coming back to see what you have to offer.

You should certainly share your affiliate links in these blogs in order to expose your audience to the products you're representing, but make sure your posts aren't commercial and not all centered around promoting products. Some types of articles that can be a good asset to your site are how-to guides, "Top 10" style lists, and posts addressing common queries and concerns that people in your market have regarding certain aspects of your niche; or latest events and trends which have come up.

Your audience wants to read authentic content that they'll want to talk about with their family and friends. If your specific niche market is beauty and health, you can cite latest studies that show the ultimate way to wash your face in the early morning, or you can share the best way to use a spray establishing on your own makeup. Presenting this kind of content allows your viewers to begin with viewing you as a specialist in your field, so when you begin mixing in product critiques or brand comparisons which contain your affiliate links they'll become more likely to trust your recommendations and buy through your link.

Whenever a consumer receives free information that they find valuable, they will reciprocate the action simply by purchasing your products. This is called the theory of reciprocity, and it's very important to many ways of creating passive income online.

Once a website is had by you or a blog to share your links on, you need to ensure that your site gets visitors. Because the internet is filled with websites, bloggers, shops, cat videos, and social press influencers, you can't depend on organic traffic only to bring audiences to your content. You'll have to increase engagement, ensure that your content shows up in queries, and build relationships together with your audience that maintain them coming back.

Collect email addresses from your own audience so you can compile an email set of people in your market. This email list is one of the greatest resources an on-line entrepreneur can have when making passive income. You can build yours by adding a sign-up package to your website's homepage with a location to enter their email address and another to enter their name. Be sure to include a free call-to-actions like "sign-up for our free newsletter" or "get linked to us" to inspire people to partake in this feature.

Offering free information products in the form of PDF files or short eBooks is also a way to gather email addresses. Customers prefer to receive free products, so they'll enter their email addresses to allow them to be sent the info. This helps you grow your email list, as well as raising the reader's openness to buying your products due to the principle of reciprocity.

Statistically, the best location for the email sign-up box reaches the top right corner of your homepage. You may also add a section with this option at the bottom of each post. These boxes ought to be linked to your email services so the addresses get preserved to your list. Then you can certainly distribute regular emails to keep in touch. These email messages can either be an email newsletter, improvements containing links to brand-new blog posts, or short emails containing tidbits of details relevant to your niche.

The theory is to create a reference to your audience. You can include your affiliate marketer links in these emails also, or just include them in posts and link the articles within the email messages. Sending out your email messages could be automated using a contact service, and you can outsource the email article marketing to a freelancer.

Featuring guest bloggers on your own site and writing because a guest on other blogs within your niche may also greatly increase the traffic to your site by exposing you to some other person's established audience. Make sure to collaborate with bloggers who have similar content, but aren't your direct competition. Their audience includes people who you know are already in your marketplace because they're following another blog page in your niche. Once you've set up an authority in your niche, you can begin sharing products as an affiliate.

An affiliate marketer network is a database of items that you can share as an online marketer. When choosing a network, you'll want to focus on what merchants are using that network and what kind of support the network provides to its affiliates. Ideally, you will want network that can be reached by phone or video chat for those who have any issues rather than one which can only become reached via email. Speak to other affiliate marketers who've worked with your potential network and look at reviews on the web from past collaborators.

You'll want to take into consideration the products that are available also. You wish to represent low-quality products or services don't, and you don't wish to be associated with false claims that may damage your credibility to your market. If the merchandise are worthwhile, check just how much commission you can make from them.

For physical products, just choose those that provide a commission of at least $40 per sale. As the manufacturing, production, and shipping and delivery of physical items costs more, the merchandise have smaller income, therefore the commission percentage you stand to create is lower.

Products with higher sale prices shall yield better commissions. These can be promoted on your site through product critiques, how-to posts, or comparisons. Share everything you like or don't like about the merchandise (and if you don't like it, get an affiliate link to an identical product and talk about it as an alternative), or share steps to make use of this product to boost their lives.

For comparison posts, your magic number is three. Discover three similar items and get an affiliate link for each. Compare the three products in your post, and offer links to each one which means that your customers feel like they possess a choice. Whichever product would offer the best profit should be featured at the top of your list. You can monitor which of the three products sells best, and feature that product prominently in something page of your site or in sidebars as a "featured favorite."

Digital items like eBooks, membership sites, or software provide higher commission percentages. These cost considerably less to produce, so they provide a very much higher profit margin. Commissions can be anywhere from 10%to 50%.

ClickBank is one of the largest affiliate networks for these digital products, & most of the products it features offer from ranging from $30 and $70. Search for products with a high gravity rating as they are in high demand and many affiliates are already generating sales with them. Your competition shall be high, but you could make a profit still. The gravity ranking on some products can be misleading if the product is newly listed. If this is the case, consider the product page's sales copy and evaluate it to competing products.

You want to select a digital product with a long sales copy that represents the merchandise well. Short sales copy doesn't convert well for this type of copy.

For goods and solutions with very high retail prices, you can accept commission percentages only 40%. This also pertains to membership applications where you receives a commission a commission each and every time the customer pays their membership fees. However, for additional digital products, the most profitable options offer commissions of 50% or greater. Cost-per-acquisition or cost-per-action applications pay a commission to the affiliate marketer for actions, not sales. These scheduled programs involve collecting zip codes, email addresses, or applications from your market. A commission of over $1 per action can make CPA applications worthwhile, but you'll want to make sure this program isn't restrictive about the way in which you promote the activities. Some of these programs is only going to enable you to promote them through mailing lists which can drastically reduce the price of engagement you'll accomplish.

When you're recommending items, stick to advertising a maximum of two or three 3 at a right time. In the event that you exceed this amount, it starts to appear more like you're pushing items on your audience and much less like you're trying to help them discover good products. People wish to trust your expert advice. To boost your credibility, it's beneficial to own and utilize the item before you advise your audience to take action.

Once your business becomes more popular, merchants may give you the product for free before you stand for it- but you might be able to get a free duplicate or sample of a product even if you're no established expert yet. You can merely inquire the merchant for a tester copy. The worst they are able to do is say "no."

Sharing a research study of your own experience with the product or compiling your thoughts on it into an honest examine will build your trustworthiness as a specialist in your specialized niche and motivate your viewers to click on the link and buy the product themselves.

Once you've found success with these two or three 3 products, you can move to featuring other products. Trying to accomplish too much at once will leave you with multiple half-done marketing promotions, that will never be worth just as much as one well-done campaign.

Amazon provides an affiliate plan called amazon Associates also. This scheduled program is normally best for bloggers who specialize in retail products or shopping-based content. This is because their visitors are already open to the idea of purchasing products at the time they're reading the blogger's suggestions. The scheduled program works like other affiliate programs. You are given an unique affiliate link which you can use to promote products, you advertise Amazon products on your own website, readers click through your link and purchase the product, and a commission is got by you.

Among the great perks of Amazon's affiliate system is that if a person buys other items from Amazon after clicking through your link, then you get yourself a commission from the entire sale and not simply the product you linked. With Amazon's vast selection of products, you also have a wider variance of products to recommend. You'll want to stick within a niche, but you can suggest a variety of products that complement one another. These can be featured in a catalog style page on your own website, in product-review-based blog posts, or in sidebars of "recommended products" throughout your website. You can even run banner advertisements imbedded with your affiliate link.

Whatever kind of product you decide to marketplace, you should spread out your links across numerous avenues. To keep track of which marketing technique converts better to sales, you can use a specialized monitoring link for each method rather than which link generates the most product sales. The links will still be unique to you, but you may use a different one for your email list than you perform in your blog post to check which link your market uses more.

If you're an Amazon affiliate you can acquire these links by likely to your account settings and clicking on "manage tracking i.d.s," in that case adding a new i.d. for every site. You can even use different links when you promote on cultural media to see how well that assists your marketing.

Live demonstrations in Facebook are a very well-known way for affiliate marketers for connecting with their audience in real time and make an individual connection which leaves customers more inclined to purchase. The second best promotion technique after live streams is usually regular video. Sharing movies on Instagram or Fb can increase engagement more than regular photos or text message posts. Posting content material onto a YouTube accounts is a more long-term strategy to vdeo sales marketing, but it can work wonders for your affiliate marketing business by increasing your credibility in your field and growing your audience.

You can also utilize these social media platforms by working paid advertisements to drive traffic to your blog or website. That is a financial investment, but the visitors can grow your audience and boost your profits. Search Engine Optimization (SEO) can help you increase traffic to your internet site without spending money on advertisements. This involves incorporating high-visitors keywords into your posts, in addition to following various other methods to increase the organic traffic your site gets from folks searching the web.

Google, for instance, will place your post higher in the serp's based on keyword utilization, the framework of your website, the relevance of your content, and the number of clicks on your own site. Keywords will be the terms internet users would type into a search bar to access your site. These should be utilized in titles, in addition to throughout your content recurrently, but you shouldn't be repetitive. This tells the internet search engine that your articles include info their users need to find.

The design of your website is considered also. A solid site structure without annoying pop-ups or a bombardment of ads shall rank higher in search results. Internet search engine algorithms also look for how often your website is back-linked by other sites. This is definitely why it could be very vital that you guest-post on other sites. When se's have their "web crawlers" looking through the internet to find the best pages, they observe how other sites send their audience toward your site often. The more frequently your website is linked, and the even more prominent the site who links to it, the more relevant you seem and the bigger up your site shall be ranked browsing results.

One mistake some affiliate marketers make isn't having their site linked the same way each and every time it's back-linked. Most of the time, your site name could be written as "www.example.com" or "example. com" and an user find yourself at your site in any event. Unfortunately, for back-linking reasons, this causes an issue. When internet crawlers come across your site through a backlink, they don't recognize these two names of domain as the same site.

If your site is listed using the "www" version five times, and the non-www version 6 times, the net crawlers will award those numbers separately to each domain rather than associating 11 backlinks to your one site. What this signifies for your SEO is certainly that you're only gaining portion of the search optimization for those backlinks, which means you should ensure that you set up which way you wish your domain to end up being written and make an effort to ensure it remains consistent. You need to improve your ranking browsing results so increased traffic comes to your website and more customers buy through your affiliate links.

Search engine optimization could be complicated. It requires a whole lot of research, and there's a learning curve certainly, but it's integral to any approach to creating passive income online. If you don't have time to learn SEO in order to increase organic visitors to your internet site, or simply don't wish to, an SEO professional can be employed on freelance websites. You can also outsource article marketing for your website as well to improve the passivity of your affiliate marketing income.

Overall, affiliate advertising is an excellent way to gain passive income because you don't have to invest financially in order to make a revenue. However, much like many methods of generating passive income, the additional money and time you're willing to invest, the greater the revenue you stand to create.

WAY 2: Amazon Self-Publishing

Creating a passive income stream takes some initial investment, whether that investment is time or money. In many cases, the task doesn't actually end once you're done with the original front loading phase because you nevertheless still need to market your business to be able to gain more income, even if you're not actively working following the first phase. One ever more popular way to create a passive income stream that doesn't require much maintenance is to publish a book. In theory, once the original function of preparing the publication is done, all you have to accomplish is collect the profits.

Amazon started out seeing that an online bookstore in the 1990s and has since end up being the second most valuable company in the globe by branching out into various areas of service. However, the company maintains its stronghold in the literary world. The Kindle Immediate Publishing (KDP) feature has created an opportunity for authors to cut out the middleman of a normal publishing house and take their item directly to customers. This allows the author to maintain 70%

of the profits from each sale- a much higher percentage than would be received otherwise- and maintain the rights with their book. For the entrepreneurially-minded, this feature to be able to distribute eBooks or paperbacks provides opportunity to create a passive income stream. The process takes quite a bit of time and effort up front, but it can pay for it over time. If you discover writing a written book too daunting, you can outsource almost every step of the procedure.

The first and arguably most important part of publishing a book with Kindle Direct Publishing is to choose the right topic. Of training course, if you're composing the written publication yourself, then you'll want to think about what personal knowledge you need to talk about and evaluate that understanding to determine whether or not it's something people are looking to learn. If you're creating a book for the purposes of earning the most money possible, you'll want release an a thing that people want to read.

Your knowledge may be well-suited to this task, or you may want to consider other topics. It's tempting to create a book based on a subject unlike any additional that is published because it will have less competition, however the risk that comes additionally is that there may not be a demand for this. At least when getting started, choose a niche that is profitable already. The competition may fiercer be, but you'll understand that there is an audience searching for books like yours already.

To choose the best niche, you'll need to do some extensive research. On Amazon's website, go to the Kindle Shop and take a look at the bestselling books. Look over the "Top 100 Paid" section in each category to find what topics people are purchasing. Each category also offers sub-categories, so you can appear at what's offering well in these too. This is where you can gain inspiration for a written book that will be profitable.

Some niches will sell well consistently, such as health, diet, fitness, self-help, and romance. In these profitable niches, many books cover the same high-demand topics. Choosing to follow the fold and cover these same topics doesn't indicate you won't make a profit as well, but you'll want to make sure you always cover rewarding topics utilizing a different approach than your competitors.

When looking through profitable niches, you'll specifically want to look out for any places where a category that's in high demand has a sub-category with less insurance coverage. Say for instance there's popular for books on healthy eating, and under that category, you find many books about intermittent fasting- but you observe that there are just a few titles that involve incorporating both intermittent fasting and a vegan diet plan. This is an example of an area where in fact the niche is rewarding and there is an insufficient coverage over a particular profitable subject matter.

Also, keep an eye out for keywords while you're looking at the best-selling books in a profitable niche. The terms that arrive more frequently are going to be conditions that are searched by customers more often. Make a list of these keywords. For example, in our previous scenario, the regularity of titles incorporating "intermittent fasting" shows that intermittent fasting is certainly a frequently searched topic. As another example, if you search in the very best 100 Paid eBooks under the category "Wellness, Fitness, & Dieting," the subcategory "Diets and Pounds Loss then, " you might see there are multiple books on the Ketogenic diet. This lets you know that there is, in fact, a demand for books on the Ketogenic diet plan. If you wanted to write a reserve for medical and dieting niche, you could jot down both of these phrases as keywords. Additional terms that will make the list would be "healthy," "fit," "fat burning capacity boost," or "weight loss." These terms are used in publication titles or subtitles in that specific niche frequently. When you choose a name for your list and book it on Amazon, you'll want to include high-traffic keywords so that you can drive more organic traffic to your reserve when customers seek out those particular words.

Once you've made a list of keywords, you should check how profitable each will end up being. This is done by looking for each keyword and assessing the results individually. As a general rule, you'll want to make sure that the search yields more than a few hundred results, but significantly less than 2,000. Too few outcomes can mean a topic doesn't have a higher enough demand, but too many results can mean that the niche is too saturated with publications currently. When you search a keyword you'll also want to observe the first page of books that arrive in the search results. For each of the books you'll have to check the publication time, Best Sellers rank, cost, author, and reviews. These details can help you determine whether or not writing a publication in this category will be feasible and potentially profitable.

The publication date of the books in a keyword search can help you gain some information regarding the niche's popularity. If most of the created books within that niche were published recently, it may mean that niche is quite profitable, but might also imply that fresh books are being released in it very frequently so it will end up being harder for your book to compete. Try to choose a specific niche market that is less inundated with brand-new releases if you would like to make a profit of your. Also, pay attention to the publication day of books if you are looking at the Best Sellers rank. New books will often receive a higher ranking from Amazon simply for being new. After two months, the books Best Retailers rank will reflect a far more realistic depiction of how the book competes. This should come into play when you're figuring out how much revenue the books in a specific niche are making every month.

The "Best Retailers rank" shows how well a book is selling out of the millions of titles on Kindle. The best-selling book on most of Amazon will have a Best Retailers rank (BSR) of 1 1 as the 10,000th most profitable book will have a BSR of 10,000 and so forth. This number is situated in the product details description when you scroll down a book's Amazon web page.

When checking out your rivals, you'll want to ensure that the very best 5 best-selling books directly in your competitive cost range ($0.99 to $3.99) of this niche are ranked between 10,000 and 100,000. A rank with a smaller number means the reserve is higher on the list of best retailers and is, therefore, selling even more copies. A true number smaller than 10,000 suggests that there is demand in this specific niche market, but it shall be difficult to compete. If multiple of the best-selling titles in a distinct segment have a rank number larger than 100, 000 it shows that there is simply not high more than enough demand for your publication to profit. A written book with a rank of 100,000 or smaller is likely making $50 to over $100 a month. You desire to pick a niche where your top 5 best-selling competitors are attracting this type of income.

When you compare books within a niche to see how yours may profit, you can overlook the books in an increased price range. Your eBook is going to be competing with books outlined at $0.99 to $3.99. These are the books that are usually produced by less popular authors or passive income creators like yourself. They may be promoted on websites or social media, but they're generally not written by well-known creators, brands, authors, or superstars. Be wary of niches that are saturated with free books also. This lowers the likelihood that consumers shall purchase yours.

Most profitable niches shall contain higher priced eBooks as well. These are usually priced around $6.99 or more, and are compiled by people who are more reputable within a specific niche. These authors are generally generating sales through traffic drawn from various promotional strategies and not simply organic visitors from keyword searches, so they don't need to be used into much concern when assessing a distinct segment.

However, it may be good for look into the top few authors that could be your competition within a niche. Run an instant Google search of the authors' titles to see if they have a big social media audience, a well-known blog page, or a brand with a large following. These authors will be driving traffic to their books also, which will make it more likely to sell better than yours. This could skew how profitable a distinct segment is apparently also. It might look like a great choice because these authors are making sales, but the sales may only be considered a direct consequence of their audience, not because of general interest for the reason that niche.

You'll also want to check the amount of reviews on the top few books in a niche. If all 5 of your top rivals have a large number of reviews, those books will show up browsing results before yours will likely. The more well-reviewed books you are competing with, the not as likely your book will get chosen by clients. Look for prospective niches where the best few best-sellers in your competitive range have got significantly less than 30 reviews.

If at least 5 of the books listed in the first web page of your keyword search results meet the requirements of a potentially profitable specific niche market then you may have found the proper concept for your book. These 5 books have to be published at least 2 months prior, have Greatest Sellers ranks between 10,000 and 100,000, be in the price selection of $0.99 to $3.99, be written by authors that are not well known, and also have less than 30 critiques each. If the market meets these criteria, you can move to selecting a topic. The marketplace will end up being well saturated with books on trending topics, so, to make the most profit, you'll likely have to put a personal spin on a trending idea. You need to create a publication that has more value for the reader than your competition's books.

You don't have to be a scholar or a trained writer to produce a book professionally. In fact, you don't even have to write the publication yourself if you don't need to, it just boils down to whether you would like to save period and invest more money, or vice versa. Writing the book yourself involves less monetary investment, but can consider a significant amount of period. Using internet freelance sites or ghostwriting companies, you can outsource the ongoing work to professionals. Freelance article writers and researchers can be found on platforms like Upwork of Fiverr. Once you have an idea for your topic, a freelance researcher can be hired to gather the required information for anywhere between $15 each hour and $50 per hour, depending on the skill amount and level of information you're looking for.

Freelance ghostwriters can be hired on a single platforms, or through websites and companies that specialize in ghostwriting eBooks. Ghostwriters can be hired for less than $0.01 per word, but remember that this can impact the entire quality of your publication. In some cases, your book may currently be formatted for eBook publishing, but it's generally a good idea to hire a professional from a freelance market in order to ensure that your reserve is usually well formatted and won't have any presentation problems when it's downloaded. It could also be beneficial to proofread your reserve yourself or hire a proofreader from a freelance site before publishing it.

Amazon presents both eBook publishing and paperback publishing with KDP. Selling your book as a paperback aswell can increase your ranking and sales. You don't even need to get worried about having copies of your book printed or kept because Amazon will printing them based on the demand for your reserve. This means that releasing both an eBook and a paperback doesn't require a lot more effort than releasing just an eBook. The paperback does, nevertheless, have an added requirement of creating a wraparound cover. Your eBook will need a cover anyway, so it that are a matter of formatting the same cover into a three dimensional version. When you have great graphic design skills, this is often done on your own. Otherwise, this could be outsourced to a freelancer as well.

Amazon provides services which make it easier to release your book without hiring freelancers, but this is often time consuming to do on your own. If you want, you can format your eBook using Kindle Create, design your own cover with Cover Creator, and preview your reserve with Kindle Previewer before publishing it. The company also provides templates for paperbacks and enables you to order proofed copies before you publish your paperback to the masses.

You can release your own eBook and begin making passive income with no financial investment if you're ready to put in the time and effort to write, edit, format, and style your book yourself. Normally, you can outsource the complete process for as little as $300. The even more you're willing to invest in your book, the better their quality will be. This can raise the amount of passive income you may make because a good reserve will get better reviews and better ranking.

You can boost your reviews through the use of pricing strategies also. In some instances, it can be good for list your publication at a price of $0 for two weeks to increase the number of downloads it gets. Clients can read your book free of charge and leave reviews so your number of evaluations grows. Then, when you've collected the right reviews over a couple of weeks, you can list your reserve at a higher price and begin making great sales.

The most famous eBook price purchased by readers is $3.99, but the most common pricings can range from $1.99 to $3.99. Make sure to cost your reserve competitively. This doesn't mean making it cheaper than the various other books in your market. Price it likewise or slightly higher to show that it's of equal or better quality.

To publish your publication, create a Kindle Direct Publishing account and enter your writer name, tax details, and payment information. Once your account is made, you'll have to list your book and enter the provided information for it in order to create something page. Besides the title and author, you'll need to put in a description of your publication also. In this explanation, you would like to really grab the reader's interest and highlight why your book is the best book available on the subject.

Upload your book's manuscript and cover, preview it, and publish it. Amazon provides support for every step of the way to assist you optimize every aspect of your reserve and provide the best product with their customers.

You can then promote your book on Amazon through paid advertisements or by supplying limited-time discount rates with Kindle Countdown Offers. Capitalizing on a few of these special offers allows your publication to be featured in regions of Amazon's marketplace that can create heavier organic visitors to your product. The original marketing of your book can take a little bit of effort, but as your book gains sales and reviews, it can improve in rank and continue getting you passive income.

WAY 3: Merch by Amazon

Another Amazon feature that will help you produce passive income is the Merch system. Merch by Amazon allows you to upload styles to be published on t-shirts and offered in the world's largest online marketplace. Amazon provides a print-on-demand assistance and order fulfillment, so you don't have to worry about creating the t-shirts, obtaining a person base, storing stock, shipping, returns, etc. They also handle all the customer service aspects. They don't even ask you for anything to sell on their platform- they just charge costs and charges on your own actual sales.

If you're no artist or designer even, you can make a profit from this ongoing service, but because of the service's popularity, Amazon has made it a bit harder to become a Merch creator. Amazon offers quality requirements to meet up and a 100% fulfillment guarantee for his or her customers, so they would like to make certain the social people offering shirts on their site are worthwhile. There's a waiting list to become among their designers, and you ought to request your invitation to use as soon as you read this and that means you don't miss your opportunity to make passive income with this service.

To be remembered as a creator, you need to request an invitation in order to apply. You'll receive your invitation when Amazon provides space for new content creators, but remember that this wait can be anywhere from a couple weeks to a year.

Once you obtain your invitation you'll fill out your application. It starts with your business get in touch with information, your social security number, as well as your bank information and routing numbers. In case you are selling shirts as yourself, not as a company, just use your own name and address. In the request type, there is a box for "more information." This package can be extremely helpful in increasing your chance of acceptance. Make hyperlinks to your style portfolio or the look portfolio of your contracted graphic designer, as well as any kind of other sites where you sell products.

If you're not going to personally design your t-shirts, tell them that. Let them know you want to outsource high-quality designs, and link the website of whatever developer you have. Suggest to them that you are a reliable business. In the web site box, link your personal or company site, or your blog.

Once you're accepted to sell your designs, you'll have to come up with good content people would want to purchase. Keep an optical attention out in public areas for what t-shirt designs you see people wearing on the streets, what keywords frequently are being used, and what phrases or image styles are being sold on t-shirts to get. Be sure to match trends on social press also, particularly Twitter, so that you can be among the first to release trend-related or meme-related content when the opportunity arises. Creating trend-related t-shirts can be strike and miss because if the demand for products exists, many creators will be releasing competing items then. But if you will be ahead of the development by being one of the first release a your products, then you can profit greatly.

You can also do key word research by looking through Amazon's Best Sellers and finding which niches appear profitable. This method follows the same manner you'd search profitable niches of eBooks, except it requires into consideration a wider spectrum of products. Using an incognito home window in your browser, head to Amazon's website and search for the most rewarding keywords in your market. Focus on the autocomplete feature and observe what other keywords customers are employing. The reason for using an incognito window is because in any other case Amazon will monitor your searches and this will alter the autocomplete outcomes. This can help you pick a profitable niche.

A few of the niches and sub-niches that are generally going to sell good are niches that people are passionate about. Types of these will be CrossFit sports athletes, vegans, social justice actions, etc. These public people want to represent their beliefs and passions publicly, so a t-shirt that suits them would sell well. When you design your t-shirt, you'll want to make sure your styles are unique and not simply copies of other styles.

Following recent events and social media styles are one method to gain inspiration for profitable merch, but there are always a couple of other ways to make a best-selling design. Evergreen designs are designs that continue steadily to sell again and again, year round. These designs have become generic usually, but they're reliable for the reason that people will want to buy them always.

Evergreen shirt designs cater to broad niches than more targeted audiences rather. Music, coffee, wine-think about how well-known these topics are on t-shirts in major suppliers. These are examples of evergreen topics you can bottom your designs off of. Holiday designs also sell well. Christmas-themed t-shirts will sell well in the fourth quarter of the year; red and pink romantic relationship themed t-shirts will sell well around Valentine's day, and so on. People prefer to show their holiday celebration and spirit through their clothes.

These three ways are great for reliable profits, nevertheless, you may also make good product sales by creating designs that focus on a specific niche, particularly for underrepresented sub-niches. For example, you could create designs for those who love cats, but a more profitable option may be to design a shirt for owners of hairless cats. Creating a nice design that's very niche can increase your sales.

Generally, the best-selling designs are not overly busy with wild colors and complicated pictures. A simple, text-based style with one very popular keyword may likely sell. Other choices are clever jokes or "inside jokes" inside your niche, logos that are not trademarked, or well-known phrases. Shirts that are designed for fans in a particular sub-market shall also sell, but it is most beneficial to design them in a way that will also be aesthetically satisfying to people beyond that specific group of fans.

Distressed-looking designs sell well but it is important to be sure that the opacity of your image is not too light when getting uploaded or it may not print well. T shirts with high-contrast colours are popular. Colorful styles with lighter colors look extremely pleasing on dark t-shirts, and, on the contrary end of the spectrum, simple designs in dark colors appearance pleasing on lighter t-shirts. In general, in the event that you don't want to make a text-based shirt, then you can certainly also sell well using pictures with active characters, simple designs, and silhouettes. The look area on Amazon's t-shirt template is certainly a rectangular area, but it's recommended in order to avoid creating designs that will print as a rectangular block.

Make sure that you don't make use of any copyrighted components, trademarked images or phrases, or any styles that incorporate someone else's intellectual property. You may use trademark checking websites to make sure your pictures and phrases are not trademarked. Be absolutely sure not to include these components because this will lead to Amazon removing your item and having marks against your account. If your accounts has multiple shirt styles removed from the Amazon marketplace, you will be banned.

Your account may also be suspended if you don't follow Amazon's content guidelines. Your shirt designs might not contain pornography, profanity, intolerant phrases, or references to traumatizing or violent events. Other reasons for suspension could be a shady activity like spending money on product reviews to increase your shirt's Best Retailers rank, creating content material descriptions that don't match your item, linking your personal blog, site, or shop, or offering quicker shipping.

Once you've come up with a couple of design concepts that you think will end up being marketable, you can create the look as a PNG image or hire a freelancer digital media professional do design it for you. Once it's designed, you'll upload it to Amazon. The image should be a PNG file with a 300 dpi (dots-per-inch) resolution and a maximum ration of 15 in . tall by 18 in . long. You'll select a t-shirt template and position your design.

If your design will not take up the whole height of the rectangular area, it is recommended to position the picture higher within the rectangle rather than centered slightly. Once it looks good, choose three colors of shirts which will look good with your style.

You can choose more or fewer shades, but three is definitely a strategic number to greatly help your customers with decision making.

Choose what sizes you would like to offer your clothing in, then create a title and explanation. Make sure to make use of multiple high-traffic keywords in your name and write a convincing explanation. Ensure that your description and title are highly relevant to the product's content and so are free of spelling errors. It can be very easy to unintentionally misspell the word "t-shirt" and end up with profanity in your name and description that causes your style to be rejected and your accounts to be at risk, so you'll desire to be extra careful to avoid that.

Once you've uploaded your design and created your item page, it's time to launch and marketplace your shirt. You can advertise your t-shirt by buying and putting on your own design, posting pictures on public media, and posting your design with your friends and family. You can also talk about photos or a link to your style in groups or forums that are linked to your niche, whether these be on Facebook, Pinterest, or various other platforms.

Once you begin making sales, your account will end up being "tiered up. " When you first become an Amazon Merch designer, you can only just upload no more than ten designs. This places you in tier 10. After you've made some sales and Amazon knows you're producing styles that people need it, you'll be upgraded to tier 25.

This allows you to market 25 designs at a right time, and so on and so forth.

If you good designs in niches where there is demand upload, Merch by Amazon can be a great opportunity to produce passive income. Plus, you keep the rights to your design, so if you discover that your styles sell well and you'd prefer to create and print your own t-shirts with the same style to market on other platforms you then don't have to worry.

WAY 4: Fulfillment by Amazon

Another Amazon feature that may build you passive income is usually Amazon FBA, or Fulfillment simply by Amazon. This ongoing provider allows you to personal your own web store without having to store your merchandise, ship out orders, or handle returns and customer service queries. You acquire your merchandise so when you list it on your Amazon seller's accounts you tell them you want customer support and fulfillment by Amazon. You will then get the address of 1 or even more Amazon warehouses where your products shall be stored, picked, and shipped when they're ordered.

You'll pay a regular storage fee to Amazon that ranges from $0.69 from January through September to $2.40, Through December october. You'll pay a picking also, packing, and handling fee for every unit that is based on how big is your product.

This method requires more of a financial investment because you do need to acquire your own stock, but it can still be used to create passive income because once your merchandise is sent off to the warehouse, you no longer have to handle any of the work to market your products in the world's largest online marketplace. If you were to handle all of this by yourself you'd need to find and purchase a place to store your inventory, process all of the orders yourself, and deal with the shipping of each individual purchase. FBA saves you time, cash and energy, as well as it allows your customers to avail of the excellent customer support that Amazon provides.

One of the best ways to sell with FBA is to create your own products. Once again, you'll want to do research to locate a profitable market. For potential niches, search the Amazon Best Retailers list and online community forums to see what items people need it.
The very best market to cater to will be a low-competition sub-niche. The top 5 items in this niche would have Best Retailers rank between 250 and 2000 and potential items that may be competing with yours, and have significantly less than 300 to 500 5-star reviews.

Ideally, the common rating about the best-selling items is 3.5 to 4 stars, and the leading item only has 150 to 250 reviews. This tells you the there is definitely demand in this niche market, but the competition is not really too much and you can become a prime competitor with an excellent selling products. You want the cost of products sold (e.g. the actual cost to create each product) to be between $3 to $10 each device, and you want to be capable to sell the merchandise for somewhere between $20 and $50 each. Essentially, you wish the cost to sell price ratio to end up being at between 10% to 15%, and up to 40%.

To choose what products to sell, look at what items are available and selling well within your niche and browse the reviews. Find out what your target customers are unhappy with regarding the products that are offered to them and also observe what they are pleased with.

You want to sell something that's in high demand with good market depth. Make use of a keyword site to check that the very best keyword for your product gets at least 250,000 searches monthly and ensure that the tenth ranked seller in your niche markets at least 300 devices per month with three to four 4 of the merchandise on the first page of a search having significantly less than 100 reviews each.

If a few of the product photos on the first web page are of low quality or not professional-looking, this is also a good sign you could be a prime competitor with this product. When you post your items, take some good quality photos of it so your listing will stick out from the rest.

Also, be sure there are no major brands catering to your niche. Your product will be able to sell at a price between $15 and $50, and that means you want to purchase from a manufacturer at a price that is between 10% and 40% of this. Simple items which won't break easily are a great wager because they are less likely to be broken in shipping and be returned to Amazon. Products should also be little enough to fit in a shoebox and weigh significantly less than 5 lbs. to avoid extra shipping costs.

If you want to offer a pre-designed product, find a wholesaler or supplier on Alibaba or AliExpress where one can purchase stock, then have it mailed to you so you can forward it to Amazon's warehouse. Or, you may order custom-designed items to have a more competitive and unique product. These can also be purchased from suppliers or manufacturers entirely on these websites. Either real way, selling with FBA involves a far more significant financial investment compared to the methods we discussed before.

If a blog is had by you, brand, or niche-specific organization, you can sell custom-branded merchandise in your specific niche market without having to handle all the orders yourself. Choose a product that customers in your niche want to buy and find a way to make it better by addressing the problems that your target clients have with existing products. Make a small portfolio of items that serve the same niche and may even be offered together. Then style a label with either an already-existing logo or one you've designed for the brand. All of the designing could be outsourced. If you don't have a genuine name for your store or brand already, you can outsource the business naming on freelance websites even.

Producers and suppliers for your products can be found on Alibaba or Aliexpress. When you decide what product you wish to make, find suppliers who sell a version of it and find if they will let you customize the product. You'll desire to be cautious about choosing a provider because you want to ensure they pay out careful attention to detail and customer support procedures, and you want to be in a position to pay easily so choose a supplier that will accept PayPal or Escrow. The very best supplier is probably not the cheapest supplier.

You also obviously want to provide a good quality product so that you can make a better profit. To test these elements, including item quality, get samples of your product from multiple suppliers. Purchase the minimum amount the supplier permits your first round of products. That real way you can gauge how well your customers like the products, and if the products are marketable before you purchase a large stock. In case you are not ordering customized products, try negotiating with your supplier to order fewer than their usual minimum order quantity even. They may be more likely to do this if indeed they don't need to put too much work into getting you the stock.

Once you've found a supplier, look at your rivals to see how you can brand and package your product to stick out. Hire a designer to create a logo, as well as a label for each product you intend to sell. Ensure that your supplier is ready to customize your product in this manner. When you post your item on Amazon, include at least 3 photos of the merchandise that showcases your logo design, and be sure to add the name of your brand or organization in the name of the product. You can register your brand with Amazon in order that other sellers won't have the ability to steal your product description, pictures, or logo.

When you cost your product, price it slightly lower than your competition initially. This can attract more initial product sales that will assist you get a better ranking on Amazon's industry and get more exposure to clients through the company's algorithm. It will also assist you to rack up evaluations which will help you improve your rankings and make your product qualified to receive Amazon's pay-per-click advertisements to increase exposure. Once some success sometimes appears by you, you can raise the price to slightly higher than your competitors.

You can also purchase a few units of inventory and send them to reputable bloggers in your niche so they can review it on their platform and boost your exposure. Once you've seen achievement with one product, launch another product to market in the same market. Launching complimentary products can help to build your brand's reputability, in addition to creating an opportunity to sell the products as a bundle which might be attractive to customers and increase product sales.

Once you've established your shop and sent your items to Amazon's warehouse, you can start making passive income without having to store your share, bother with shipping, or deal with any returns or customer service issues.

Another method of offering with Amazon's FBA assistance is normally by doing retail arbitrage. This calls for a more substantial investment of time but makes it possible for a smaller expenditure of cash. Retail arbitrage involves purchasing sales at shops in your region to acquire products at discounted prices. Then, you list these products on Amazon at their primary price or a slightly discounted price that still enables you to make a profit. Afterward you send your products to Amazon and invite them to handle the rest. This could be profitable because product sales and deals at major retailers vary by area, so the customers purchasing online might not have access to that item at the discount you bought it for.

Combining these sales with couponing makes it possible for you to buy large levels of items for a very low price that will increase your profit margins. You can even purchase items in mass at warehouse stores like Sam's Club at a minimal price per unit, sell them individually online for a profit then. Customers of Amazon will generally haven't any issue paying full price or nearly a high price simply for the capability of having the item delivered to their home instead of going to a retailer themselves.

One profitable method to approach retail arbitrage is to get large levels of goods that are only obtainable in your region. This gives online shoppers who reside in other parts of the world a chance to buy items that may not be obtainable to them in their local stores.

Fulfillment by Amazon could be a great way to create passive income because once your merchandise is in the warehouse, all you have to do is relax and collect the profits. It does help continually market your products and update your shop, but it's your decision how much effort you wish to put in. Amazon may be the largest online industry in the world, so your products will be available to an enormous customer base which increases the potential for profit. Like with almost every other passive income possibilities just, the more money and time you're ready to invest in your FBA store, the greater your opportunity to make money.

You can even use FBA together with other online stores if you are selling products from your own website. You can process your sales through your own website and pay Amazon $5.95 to deliver the order from their warehouse so you still won't need to bother with paying for space to shop your goods, nor spend energy and period to ship them out.

WAY 5: Online Programs

Another smart way to create passive income is to share your knowledge and expertise with others via online programs. As with most internet sites, it's helpful to have an established popularity or brand that holds you as an authority in your specific niche market. This can be made up of a blog or a website, and can almost always increase the amount of profit you may make online. Creating an online training course can add to your professional status by proving that you know what you're talking about with regards to topics in your field.

Your established reputation might help sell your course, and your course might help solidify your reputation. It's a win-win. Online programs are also one of the most profitable ways to make passive income online. Creating one requires an investment of at least a couple of months, but the return on investment is generally high, and a well-made training course can also lead to a far more loyal market and increased traffic to your site, blog, affiliate marketer links, or online store.

To build your training course, you need to choose a topic you are knowledgeable about first, passionate about, and have encounter in, whether life experience of formal teaching. You don't need to be a scholar on the subject, nevertheless, you should share information that's valuable to people who are less acquainted with it and present an unique and helpful perspective.

If your knowledge isn't necessarily highly relevant to a profitable niche, make an effort to incorporate your experience and knowledge right into an unique perspective on a thing that is profitable. You want to select a topic that people are not only discussing but that they are asking questions about. To create money, you need to teach what folks want to learn. Every other on the web instructor is thinking the same thing, therefore they'll likely be creating classes in similar niches. Your course will have to set itself apart by within the gaps in the info the competition is offering. It shall still need to be similar enough to guarantee the demand for it exists, but your course must provide value to the student that other courses usually do not. When you promote your training course, you shall include this distinction in the description so people understand why you're the best option.

Once you've chosen your course topic, you'll need to decide what materials to involve in your course content. This will include only the material that is important in acquiring the desired learning outcome and nothing at all else. Most importantly, make sure to include content that fills the areas where the competition falls short.

A program that is created for a targeted sub-niche gets the potential to be more profitable when compared to a generalized course. For instance, a course titled How exactly to Create a Spreadsheet may have significant competition, whereas a course titled How exactly to Create a Spreadsheet in Google Sheets addresses a subject that may have less competition and popular. Also, keep in mind, a long course will not translate to a valuable course necessarily, and your students might struggle to stick to a course full of unnecessary information.

For a profitable course, a 2-3 3 hour course comprising multiple 20 to 30 minute modules will be ideal, and it must be priced higher than the competition slightly. Of course, because you're pricing it higher you need to ensure that it is packed with value. Prices your course lower than your competitors' helps it be appear as though your course is much less valuable and could actually reduce your sales.

Once you've decided what details you wish to use in your course, framework the program modules to follow an all natural progression and achieve the required learning results. Similar designs and ideas could be collected into module groups. Then, the basic ideas within those modules ought to be organized in a way that flows logically. Simple, concrete truths should be explored before shifting to more abstract ideas, and the topic matter should segue perfectly from one topic into another.

In classes that are job-oriented, the information should follow the actions of the real job environment. In all full situations, each lesson should build upon the previous details to bring the college student closer to the required mastery of the topic. This information should be presented in various methods to accommodate all aspects of adult learning. Information can be represented in photos visually, videos, or illustrations, and also through reading articles, journaling, multiple-choice quizzes, self-evaluations, and other practical methods. Video may be the most commonly used and broadly respected way of relaying information, nevertheless, you can incorporate any methods that are well-appropriate to your unique topic.

Next, you'll need to produce your content. Videos are the most popular and the very best teaching method presumably. These can be recorded in another of 3 ways: lecture style, with a green display screen, or with a screen recording.

Lecture style movies showcase the teacher explaining the concept to the camera, sometimes with a white board to pull or write things out. With a green display screen, the teacher continues to be in the frame explaining the concept, but pictures, slideshow slides, or animation could be added in the background through the editing stage to better illustrate the principles. Screen-castings show a recording of the teacher's screen as they go through whatever techniques they're explaining, plus a small video package in the corner that presents a webcam video of the teacher.

You can choose which design of video is best suited to your topic. After it's recorded, you can edit your video yourself or you can outsource the video editing to a freelancer. Video editing software program costs a few hundred dollars, so either real way, you will need to invest some cash in this step. Any worksheets, checklists, or other paperwork you wish to include together with your course should be uploaded as PDF data files in order to be conveniently printed or downloaded.

There are a few ways to boost your profits by adding value to your course. Including downloadable assets like worksheets, checklists, templates, and video lessons gives your students more value for their money. Offering one-on-one coaching or group training creates an opportunity for your college students to acquire more knowledge from you in an individualized manner, while creating a possible income stream also. The income from coaching wouldn't normally be passive income, which means this is optional absolutely, but it does validate your expert position and promote your program.

You can host live calls or webinars together with your students also, or create an exclusive Facebook group where you help your students create a community of individuals interested in the same topic. Other ways give yourself an advantage over the competition include being available by phone or email to greatly help students with questions and supplying a certificate of completion upon finishing the course.

Your course could be designed and sold using a learning management program (LMS) like Teachable. This type of platform will help you through the process of building your training course from scratch. You can import your PDF documents, photos, and videos from your own Google Travel or Dropbox, and quickly arrange it into your course with templates. You can also create a new website for your course if you don't curently have one and Teachable will take treatment of the hosting and give you a free of charge domain name. Both your website and course will be mobile friendly. If you already have a website, you can hyperlink your course to your site and run it from generally there while still having your LMS take care of signups, payments, and tracking metrics like completion rates or student demographics.

You can sell your course within an online course marketplace like Udemy also. This is a less rewarding option generally, but it could be great if you're trying out your first course, or as a real way to draw increased traffic to your LMS hosted course. Online course marketplaces provide a template and hosting providers to build your training course, or you are allowed by them to upload your own. Once it's uploaded, they have the proper to price and market your course because they wish. This may mean your program gets given away for free or sold for an extremely low price. That is why it's recommended to create a shorter, more condensed edition of your course to list in on the web marketplaces.

The mini-course ought to be packed with enough value to entice potential learners, but shouldn't contain more info than you'd discharge on your own blog or website free of charge. By the end of your market mini-course, add in a reward module that encourages learners to take the "advanced" training course you have on your website. This will send out them to your full, LMS hosted course. You might still gain some income from the marketplace course, but it ought to be used generally

Once your program is ready to be sold, you'll need to choose a cost. Prices too low for your course shall make it show up less valuable to potential students. Pricing as well high may necessitate you to reduce prices later on, which doesn't look good either. If you want to produce a profit, you should not sell your training course for under $50. If you want to maximize your profits really, you should mark it over $200.

When you're starting out with your first program, you can start with your pricing about the lower side and steadily increase it until your sales start showing some level of resistance. Keep in mind that you need to price your course based on the worthiness it holds, not on its duration. Those who are purchasing these high-quality courses could likely learn the majority of this information for free somewhere on the web, but they want to get it from a specialist without needing to search all over for this. Your course ought to be shown as the high quality value course, so that it should be priced higher than the competition slightly. This higher pricing will attract serious students who really desire to learn what you are teaching and you will be more likely to put into action the knowledge and skills they gain. They are the people you would like to market your course to.

In your sales copy, describe what credentials you have that makes you an professional, whether it be through life experience or formal training, and what learning outcomes your students can get. In detail, outline the problem they are facing to show you realize their pain and problems, then propose a graphic of the world where this problem is fully gone (the world after they've completed your course), to make a contrast between the full life they have and the life span they can achieve. Then explain how your training course will get them to this ideal place- how will they feel different at the end of the course, exactly what will they have learned to do, and how will they reap the benefits of this change in their life or career.

You can put a number on the information also. For instance, you can illustrate the money they conserve by learning from you rather than taking classes at a college, traveling to seminars, or employing personal coaches. Your college students want to observe how your program shall transform their lives. Presenting your course such as this and charging an effective amount of money will attract students who certainly are a right fit for this. This will leave you with fewer refund requests, higher satisfaction prices, and higher completion prices.

Another method of pricing your course is certainly to create three versions of it at different cost points and offer them in a sort of "basic," "superior," and "deluxe" fashion. The basic course will be the same condensed version you released in course marketplaces. It's mainly the same info you'd release free of charge, with just a little added worth. This course is priced suprisingly low because it doesn't present much worth.

The second pricing option for the course, our "premium" course, contains the course you need to sell. This is the full training course as you wish to present it to students, and it's costed significantly higher than the basic course.

The 3rd pricing option provides the "deluxe" course, which is merely the center course with a tiny bit extra offered really. This option is priced greater than the middle course significantly, but it only offers a little bit more value. This added value is actually a collection of templates and worksheets or PDF of some extra information. The point of the high-priced option isn't to sell, it's actually to operate a vehicle your client toward the "premium" package containing the actual training course. Psychologically, people like to make choices, so when they're selecting one option out of three that are a valuable deal, they will have an easier time rationalizing the buy.

Happy customers will be more likely to share your course with their friends, which increases your course's exposure. You may also increase your course's exposure with paid advertisements, email blasts, and social mass media posts. In the event that you don't have an email list extensive enough to promote your training course with email blasts sufficiently, you can go after a jv partnership with a more established person or firm in your target market. This partnership allows a person or business with a larger email list (and with it, the founded trust of their viewers) to promote your course with their email list in exchange for a share of the profits from any resulting product sales. Because this payment only takes place as a commission if sales are made, this is free advertising essentially. A respected authority within your niche has now lent you credibility to an market made up entirely of individuals within that specific niche market without any financial purchase from you.

However, if your program is costed to low, these partners might not want to vouch for you as the commissions won't be worthwhile for them. A 40% commission on a $90 sale is usually a considerably lower incentive than a 40% commission on a $900 sale. That is yet another good reason why pricing your course well is important.

To find jv partners, first look within your network. Look for someone who has usage of an audience within your marketplace or who offers connections to somebody with an identical audience. This is actually the best avenue because people who know you, know very well what you present, and currently like and trust you are more likely to be willing to attest to you. People within your viewers, email list, and customer base may possess connections that could benefit you also.

If you can't look for anyone connected to your network closely, search for prominent influencers or bloggers in your market. Bloggers are generally ready to promote affiliate items for a commission, so your course can be made up of those products. You can approach podcasts inside your niche also, authors of books your target customers are buying, and hosts of industry occasions or conferences.

You may also approach instructors of online courses within your niche, just not your direct competition. Offer them free usage of your training course and let them choose if they would like to promote it. Because they've received something for free, they might be much more likely to wish to accomplish a favor for you in return, and that's quite definitely what you're asking them to accomplish: a favor.

Promoting a stranger's program or product to an viewers you've established a trusting relationship with is not an opportunity that everyone would leap at. Before you ask you to definitely become your joint venture partner, establish a relationship with them and increase value to them. Buy their items, leave a positive review of their reserve, refer someone to them, or sign up to their email list. By helping them and showing an appreciation for the worthiness they bring, you can develop an actual friendship to build a continuing business partnership on.

Building relationships with influencers in your niche grows your networking and can positively effect your business in the long run. Write them a customized email introducing yourself, complimenting them on specific areas of their work that you appreciate. After that tell them which you have a course you imagine would complement their products or services and their market may enjoy, so you'd prefer to discuss going after a joint-venture partnership and you'd like them to get in touch with you if they're interested. If they're, schedule an in-person meeting or, at the minimum, a phone contact rather than continuing over email so you can have a more personal interaction.

If you decide to pursue a partnership, outline the agreement in detailed composing and clarify it with them before completing the conversation. Make a very clear and simple agreement on paper, then produce an affiliate link to allow them to share and proceed together with your joint venture partnership.

The initial creation of your web course may require a substantial time investment, and it can need a financial investment to outsource different elements of the procedure, but there is vast potential to profit off of such an electronic product. Once your program is available on the internet, you don't need to do much else. The marketing could be outsourced even. Overall, this is an excellent method to create passive income.

WAY 6: Network Marketing

Network marketing is also referred to as multi-level marketing or direct sales. In this business style, an independent distributor or representative earns income by selling a product or assistance for a commission. The representative can earn commissions for recruiting new representatives also, as well as receive a percentage of the gains from any product sales these recruits make. This method is among the most misunderstood methods to make passive income widely, but it can be quite effective. It does need a fairly minor monetary investment of a few hundred dollars up to couple thousand dollars and a fairly significant investment of amount of time in the beginning, but once you've grown your business it could get you passive income.

Multilevel marketing is often confused with a pyramid scheme, but the two are actually different. First of all, pyramid schemes are unlawful. They involve recruiting brand-new participants and needing them to pay out an investment. The brand new recruit is then told to bring in more traders and they'll get money when each one invests. This payment is received in the event that you recruit, and the money filter systems up the pyramid. Some network marketing businesses do resemble these schemes, which means you need to be cautious of these- but network marketing differs from pyramid schemes since it offers a genuine goods and services for sale.
A good network marketing company will have a chance for marketers to make money also without recruiting. Reputable companies will participate the Direct Selling Association (DSA) or the Association of MULTILEVEL MARKETING Professionals (ANMP).

When choosing a network marketing company to utilize, it's important to consider multiple factors. Because you're offering to your personal network, the business and products you represent will get in touch with your own personal reputation. Look at the company's values and the objective the founders stand by. Consider whether or not these ideals resonate with you and if this company is something you would like to align yourself with. Also, consider the goods and services you would be selling. Is it something you'd want to talk about with your friends and family? Is it something you'll use and believe in?

Avoid companies that utilize "front end loading" by requiring their representatives to get a large inventory to sell. These ongoing businesses generally make most of their sales with their personal consultants and distributors, and there isn't really much cash to be made with them. Be certain the ongoing company you choose wants you to market products a lot more than they push you to recruit, and that the products are worthwhile enough so that you can be willing to get them even without the chance to make income. Products also needs to be unique, competitively priced, and serve a want that exists in the prospective market. They are service level factors to check out when narrowing down which multilevel marketing companies may prove to be worthwhile. Once you've got a shorter list, consider the deeper aspects of the firms to find one that's right for you.

If the merchandise are something you would stand by, have a look at how the ongoing company makes them. Companies that manufacture their own items are more deeply invested in the standard of their products and their customers' knowledge, and also in pricing their products more reasonably. When a company outsources the creation of their products, the maker doesn't necessarily have any personal concern for the standard of the merchandise. Outsourcing also increases the chances a competing company would be able to obtain ahold of the products' formulas and release very similar competing products.

As for profit, outsourcing the items' manufacturing means the business needs to make enough profit from the product sales to cover this expenditure and pay commission with their representatives, and still make their personal money. It isn't really a deal breaker for you personally as a marketer, however the pricing is likely to be less competitive in this full case.

You'll also want to make sure that the business values their retail customers doubly, and the retail sales of the merchandise are a crucial section of the company's business plan. Businesses that require new recruits to purchase large amounts of share don't make the majority of their product sales from retail sales to regular customers. An excellent company will have a product their marketplace can benefit from without needing to turn into a distributor of the product.

Almost all network marketing businesses (around 90%) fail within 3 years. When these companies fail before you possess a chance to build your business, you're left without profit and perhaps even significantly less than you started with. For this reason you'll want to find a network advertising business that has been working for at least three or so years with a successful product and still has momentum.

To determine if the company is going strong or if you've currently missed your chance, look at how they conduct business. Dig around and figure out whether the firm owns their personal headquarters or just rents office space. This gives you a concept of their stability. Do they possess a minimal debt load? The ideal company does not have any debt, but provided that your debt load is less than 25% of total possessions it can still be a great choice. Do they have an administration team, live customer service, and positive cashflow after expenses? Do they offer their marketers with tools to help market the merchandise? Many good network marketing companies have great tools to help you be successful with their business.

If these things check out, check out the owners. Check if the current owner of the business was previously involved with any failed multilevel marketing companies. If they possess, it's a reddish flag-nonetheless it doesn't have to be a hard "no" exclusively for that reason. If they've been associated with multiple failed multilevel marketing businesses, however, do not get involved.

The very best companies to work for are family-owned with multiple family members directly committed to the function of the company. These kinds of companies are more likely to be dependable on the long term, and less likely to be marketed to new owners. When companies like these change hands, however, it generally doesn't bode well for marketers. Look for a business that is more likely to keep being profitable for a while.

Once you've found a firm you want to work with and the merchandise you would like to represent, it's period to launch your network marketing business. As the buy-in rates are very low and you 'must' have any experience in operating the business don't, many people perceive the working of a network marketing business as equivalent to joining a club. This mindset, nevertheless, will be detrimental to your success.

If you were opening a traditional store, you'd help to make a large financial investment in addition to invest years of your life into learning how exactly to work a business. You'd build your business from the ground upwards, and it might be tough for the first couple of years while you're struggling business grew- but you'd power through and keep your attention on the prize. It might take 18 to two years for your business to start showing a profit, but you'd keep pressing because you'd worked hard for it.

When you open a multi level marketing, however, your initial expense is a lot, much lower. You don't possess as much on the line, so you're not as motivated to keep pushing forward. The issue with this lack of motivation is a network marketing business is still a continuing business, and it will take time to grow still. In order to be successful, you should look at your business in the right light. Start your business with a grand starting, the same way you would if you were opening a physical store.

Don't mentally consider network marketing as a real business just, treat it as such. Create a business cover yourself that includes how much you can or will spend money on startup costs and one year's operating costs. If you do that before joining a network marketing company, this assists you ensure that any financial expenditure you have to make is at your budget.

It can be helpful to find another also, more experienced internet marketer in your area who may become your mentor and assist you to set your business up for achievement. They can introduce you to their network, assist you to establish yourself, and teach you how to sell your item and recruit new consultants effectively. Someone in the neighborhood area and can meet with you personally is ideal, but getting someone online who can mentor you over the phone or video call may also be helpful. There are also online language resources to assist you gain training in multilevel marketing to build your business.

When you're starting out, create a business intend to be sure you're viewing your business with the proper mindset and gain a solid knowledge of what you're aiming for. Business plans are often created for submission to banking institutions or potential traders- which you'll likely not be doing- but it is still a good tool in establishing your brand-new business.

Start with an ongoing business description that explains what exactly your business does, what makes it stand out from your competition, and who also your target individuals are. Next, analyze your marketplace. Research who your competition are, who your potential customers are, and what exactly are the styles happening in your sector. Detail the organization of your business after that.

If you're investing with companions or outsourcing components of the work, define what role each individual plays in the procedures of the continuing business. What skills do they bring to the desk, what duties do they possess, and how their involvement is in the operations. Following this, look at the product or service you are available and outline what exactly it is, why you are selling it, how your visitors will benefit from it, and the full lifestyle cycle of the product. Address how you will market your products and increase your profits, then enter the financial projections including how much cash you can realistically make selling this product. Take note of just how much time you will invest in the project on a regular basis, your projected income, as well as your projected expenditures. When this is completed, compile a listing of your business plan.

Once your business is set up, you'll have to start it and market your products. Be sure you are aware and knowledgeable of any relevant analysis or studies regarding your items and know your products thoroughly enough to handle any questions or doubts your visitors may have about them. You should become a specialist on anything you're going to represent. Host a get in your home together, at a hotel, or in a meeting room to share information regarding your business and expose the goods you are available to potential customers, but don't make it too much like a sales page. End up being confident and concise, providing a brief overview of what your company is, why you're component of it, and what's great about the product you're providing. Add a couple of testimonials, preferably from people you know or have met individually, and show the merchandise.

Share the necessary information, allow your visitors to ask questions if they'd like then. Giving too much information through the initial display can seem like you're shoving something at them instead of offering them a thing that will be beneficial to their lives.

You can host a virtual launch in conjunction with your in-person event also. This can be either on your day of, or your day after your in-person launch and should take place on your own business's Facebook page. Distribute the invites from your personal Facebook, give incentives for involvement, and follow up with an individualized message something along the lines of:

"Hey, _____. You were sent by me an invite to my online launch party! It'll only take a short while of your time and you'll get a reward just for viewing the live stream. I think you'll like what I'm sharing. I got involved with the corporation for (brief summary of explanations why) cause and the products have helped me in __ way. I believe it would be good for you because it could help with __ issue you're having, why not just hop on the live stream and hear what it's about?"

After that, in your live stream, share your reasons for being a part of the network marketing organization and explain the company's story, and what it is about their ideals or products that drew you into working with and representing them. Speak briefly about the opportunity the business provides with multilevel marketing, and talk about a few success stories of customers who've used the merchandise and of marketers who have found achievement with their business.

End the video with a proactive approach that encourages your viewers to check out up with you. This is when your incentive comes in handy, and you could say something like:

"Message me which means you are known simply by me were watching, and I can send you ___ reward." If they message you, ask follow-up questions to get feedback on the release, your business, and what your customers think of the merchandise. This can help you find out what issues and questions your visitors have surrounding your products, so you consist of those in your information in the years ahead. This follow-up is also a great time to pitch your business as a choice to potential distributors who may grow your network."

You can market your products via social media outlets also, a blog, a website, or an email list. It could be a good idea to create specific pages for your multi level marketing separate from your main blog, website, or social press accounts. On these pages, you can talk about your personal reviews, success stories of clients and distributors, and information regarding your products or the chance to function for your network marketing company.

One web page of your network marketing internet site should explain who you are, what you do, who your services or products can help, and how your services and products are helpful. On this page somewhere, there should be an application for prospective customers to request more information about your products. There also needs to be a separate, but similar type, for potential representatives to request more info about joining your business. This allows you to grow two email lists to which you reach send out specialized email blasts.

Your business may also need a Facebook page. Because Facebook gets the most daily active users, it's the very best social media platform for network marketing. This page ought to be specifically for your multi level marketing and should link to your website to drive traffic. It will share information that adds worth to your niche and in the passions of your target market, and it should definitely not always be specific to your product. Remember, you're attempting to build associations and trust together with your customers so they will have a chance on the products you represent.

Creating groups designed for your customers allows people in your target market with comparable interests to talk to each other and create a community. You can facilitate this relationship building by publishing questions or games that are highly relevant to your item or niche. Gaining a large following is great and will spread the word about your business, but it's not almost as important as having great engagement and a trusting relationship with the proper audience. Than creating a business with a wider reach rather, create a business with a deeper connection to the potential representatives and clients who will vouch for your products. In network marketing, an included network is even more profitable than a large, impersonal one.

Your individual Facebook profile should not mention your multilevel marketing, but you may use it to connect to people in your network with personalized direct communications directly. Each of these messages should add value to the lives of your possible client. Start by asking them about latest events within their lives. After that, when you mention your business, do therefore in a manner that tells them why you think the products is actually a positive addition with their lives, or how about the opportunity to utilize your company seems just like a good suit for them. After that you can invite them to become component of your business Facebook web page or have them give you their email addresses to learn more. Stay away from being "salesy" or industrial and make each message as customized as possible.

You should purchase a business card with your photo also, business name, email, phone number, and website link on it so that you can give it to people you meet in person. This way you can inform them enough about your product or business to interest them just, and you can end up being contacted by them to ask questions later.

Network marketing will help you create a blast of passive income by establishing your brand and presence inside your market and becoming a trusted resource for products and info for your customer base. You may make the early areas of business growth more passive by outsourcing this content creation for your website and social media web pages, but multilevel marketing builds on your personal network, so you will have less possibility to outsource other aspects of the procedure. Once you've recruited plenty of distributors on your team and created a person base of recurring customers, your network marketing income shall require much less effort.

When your business has reached critical mass, your items and firm will speak for themselves. Your business shall continue steadily to grow and make sales without your dynamic participation. The key to reaching this aspect is finding dedicated distributors to add to your team and become sure you've chosen a product or service that can speak for itself and gain recurring, loyal clients. To grow a team of dedicated, hard-working leaders, you need to be a devoted, hard-working leader. Your attitude and power toward your business will established the tone for the type of team you build, and that'll be what determines your achievement in creating passive income through network marketing.

WAY 7: Blogging

Blogging is among the best ways to build an online business which can be monetized. If you haven't noticed right now, a blog is crucial to maximizing income across almost every method of creating passive income. Whether it's a way to share your affiliate marketer links, or an accepted place to promote your web course and grow your email list, a well-design blog is a huge asset to any web business. Maintaining a blog has the potential to become time consuming, but you can outsource nearly every aspect of the process to freelancers, from choosing a genuine name and building a website to creating the blog's content. Your blog is a good place to connect with your audience by providing them valuable information for free and establishing yourself as a specialist within your niche.

When you're creating content, it needs to be informative, entertaining, and real. Your site may be centered around sharing beneficial information, nonetheless it shouldn't read just like a boring lecture. End up being personable and write the same way you'd speak in a discussion (or have your freelancer write that method) so your readers feel more deeply connected to your content. These types of posts are more likely to inspire readers to talk about them on social media or send them with their friends.

Share perspectives on recent trends or events inside your niche, studies that are relevant to your subject material, "Top 10 10" design lists, and how-to guides. You can, and certainly also needs to incorporate the products you sell, paid promotions, affiliate marketer links, etc., but you want to encounter as if you're sharing a product with a friend- a thing that will advantage their lives, and not like you're a salesperson attempting to turn a profit. The massive amount valuable free information you provide can make your readers much more likely to want to buy you items when you do share them.

Building this kind of relationship with your audience enables them to appreciate the worthiness you bring to their lives and trust your suggestions. You should also make sure to constantly inform your audience if you stand to profit from any activities they take on your website, whether it be clicking on buying or ads products from a link. Again, the even more your audience trusts you, the even more loyal a person base you'll have.

As mentioned many times in this book, creating an email list is a huge asset to your online business. This enables you to send out your posts, products, and updates right to an audience of individuals who have already expressed curiosity in your business or your niche. You can automate your email messages for up to weeks beforehand using a contact system that can send out text messages en masse to your entire list. These systems can be used to manage your email list also, track leads, track opt-in rates, track open up rates, track click-through rates, etc. This can be a great service really, but it's vital that you ensure your emails are just as you want them before they're sent. If your email consists of a glaring mistake, it will be broadcast to everyone on your own list and this can make you lose sales or subscribers. Double-check that there are no typos, incorrect info, or damaged links before you setup a contact for publication.

You can grow your email list in various of ways. Generally, you want people to sign up voluntarily. This lets you know that these folks are interested in what your blog has to present and also lets you know that your list can be full of clients who are in your target market. Your website should include a sign-up box in the very best right corner of your website's homepage, as well as at the bottom, middle, or side of each post. This box should simply have an area for the email address, an area for the customer's name, and a switch that says "subscribe."

You could incentivize potential customers to join up by giving them a special packet of free bonus information. This can be a compilation of past blog posts that are edited together to flow perfectly in a PDF file, or it could be a brief eBook or educational video. If they opt-in to the offer, they provide their email address to allow them to be sent the product. This incentive can be presented in a banner over the top of your website, in a pop-up in the bottom corner of your site, or anywhere else that it is found by you will be the right addition to your blog's content.

You can collect emails with a "landing page also. " This page will pop up when a visitor enters your website. It should be basic, and all it should contain is a space to enter your email, an area to enter your name and an indicator up button. If it's a pop-up, it will also provide the choice to click away without entering an email address, but this should not really be easy or prominent to recognize.

To make passive income with your blog, you may use it mainly because an advertising tool to promote your other passive incomes streams. Supplying eBooks and other information products can allow you to create an almost pure profit if you compile the information yourself. You can come up with a collection of blog posts you've created and stitched the information together, then put in a bit of valuable information that wasn't previously included and publish it as an eBook. It doesn't need to be long, and it will be worthwhile for your visitors to purchase because they are able to access the info in a single easy form rather than searching around for this. You may also create manuals or reports if they are highly relevant to your niche. Digital goods certainly are a great way to obtain passive income as the profit margins are high, however the investment of time and energy can be extensive.

If you don't desire to create your own digital products, you can still revenue off of the demand for these goods by offering other companies' products as an affiliate marketer. As stated earlier, sharing products or services that can be purchased by other companies can develop passive income by generating you a commission of every sale you generate for them. Digital information products generally bring a much higher commission because the income are higher. You can share these with your viewers to create an opportunity for them to find out about topics in your niche from a specialist source besides yourself.

To improve traffic to your blog and improve your odds of affiliate sales, put your blog wherever your target clients traffic frequently, such as for example Reddit forums, sociable media hashtags, or Facebook groupings within your niche. Share your blog post in these areas, and let your audience come to you. You can also increase traffic by being actively involved with these forums or groups so potential customers begin to notice you and gain curiosity in checking out your site. Different ways to approach affiliate marketing and create passive income are detailed previously in this written publication.

As you may have noticed, Amazon is a prime device (zero pun intended) for creating passive income online, and affiliate marketing is no exception. Amazon Associates, the company's affiliate system, allows users to link to items listed on Amazon and gain a commission on sales produced through their links. This program also enables affiliates to generate a commission on any various other products that are ordered through Amazon after a customer clicks through their links, and continue steadily to profit from any purchases that customer produces up to 15 days afterward. This is an excellent affiliate program to get commissions from, but it is most effective to bloggers who reveal shopping, merchandise, or retail products already. Readers of these blogs already are more inclined to make purchases, therefore the likelihood that they'll purchase through the blog's links is certainly greater than other readers.

You can monetize your blog using Google AdSense also. This entails displaying Google advertisements on your website, so when a visitor clicks through the advertisement you get a percentage of the advertisement costs that the advertised organization paid. The advertisements Google displays on your blog are highly relevant to your site's content, so they cater to your niche and raise the likelihood that readers shall actually click through.

To get started, you'll want a Google account and a blog page to host ads on, in addition to a phone number and the mailing address associated with your money (so you can create payment). Google will check that your website offers useful, original, and relevant articles that brings value to its readers. In addition they turn to see if your site is clear in what you stand for, what topics you post about and what worth your articles brings to your audience. Your contact information ought to be readily available in an easily accessible part of your website, the whole site ought to be mobile friendly, and the website should not have pop-up advertisements which certainly are a nuisance to users and prevent them from savoring a pleasant website viewing experience.

Google ads additionally require that you will be upfront about why you collect visitors' private information and what will be achieved with said information, along with clarifying which links on your sight are sponsored clearly. Your blog may also have to include a privacy policy that informs audiences when third parties could be using and reading cookies on the users' browsers or collecting information with web beacons. Their ads could also not be displayed online that violate the laws of copyright or link to sites that violate the laws of copyright. Their list of specifications is longer, but it's not unreasonable. A well-made, respectable blog may likely easily fit these criteria.

Your blog is a superb way to grow your following and establish yourself as a trusted authority in your field. Once your followings have grown, you can begin making passive income off of your site easily. It shall be an integral element in maximizing profits in other businesses, and there is no limit to the amount of cash you may make through blogging and your online business. If you want to take a more active role in making money off your site, you can even offer one-on-one coaching to your readers to allow them to get personalized expert advice and answers to their questions if they pay you a fee.

What things to send to your email list? Email newsletters filled with useful content. Short, quick-to-read emails (folks are active). Links to video clips with useful articles. Announcements of item launches. Industry news as well as your commentary. Sales offers. A mix of "editorial" content, product sales offers, product launches, affiliate gives. Editorial content-developments in your industry, best practices in your niche, ideas, inspirational story of previous customers.

Free info is a tease for paid products. Use engaging subject matter lines that grab interest and compel the reader to click. Obtain whitelisted- in your initial email, send instructions to the subscriber to add you to their set of trusted emailers so you don't get considered a spammer and get banned. Mix in sales gives with useful content

You can't pitch each day. Find a very good times of day to send messages to your list. Determine this by tests what your open rates are in different times, run the winner then. Make emails mobile friendly, this option comes in most email delivery programs.

Offer low-cost introductory items first- your front side end. Offer customers steadily higher-priced products. Fewer people buy costly products, therefore bring people in to increase the probability of a purchase continually.

WAY 8: Shopify

Shopify is an online eCommerce platform that essentially lets you work your own online retail store. The website offers over 100 templates to create your store, many of which are provides and free of charge themes designed for stores in specific industries like jewelry, electronics, or fashion. You can customize each theme which means that your store is unique, and also add fonts, colors, as well as your personalized logo to create a shop that represents your online brand.

Hosting the store requires a paid subscription, therefore there is some monetary investment. You can outsource the building of the website if you want also. Subscription plans come in three different levels; a $29 Basic strategy that also pays 2.9% and $0.30 of each transaction to Shopify; a $79 Shopify program that pays 2.6% and $0.30 per transaction; and a $299 Advanced plan that pays 2.4% and $0.30 per purchase. The Basic package is plenty enough to get started on your first Shopify store, and you may upgrade if you want later. The regular Shopify Advanced and strategy plan offer additional reporting tools, but the primary cause users switch to these programs is because they provide greater amounts of file storage.

If you would like to sponsor a Shopify store, your first step is to join up and create it. You shall need an email, a password, and an unique store name. You'll have to give them information about yourself also, including your name, country of residence, address, phone number, and desired products type you wish to offer. Once your accounts is established you'll start developing your shop. Filter through themes by industry, features, reputation, or price until you find the main one you want, then go through the sample image to check on the reviews of additional store owners who've utilized this theme and see if it's cellular friendly. If it's up to standards, change it to your liking. Modifying Shopify themes is simple and can be achieved without coding, or you can outsource this to a professional if preferred. You can upload your personal logo, reposition product pictures, display social media buttons, add slides to a carousel on the homepage, and customize the looks of the products in your collection web pages. Once your website is structured how you want to buy, you can list your items.

Now, let's focus on selling products on Shopify via affiliate marketer links to make passive income. Products could be added to your shop from the administration area of your account. You shall upload images and write a product description for every product. If you're using an affiliate link, you may use pictures from the merchant's site, but it may be better to take your very own professional quality photos of the product if possible. This means that the photos on your own store page look cohesive by all becoming the same measurements and quality. Once your images are uploaded, write a detailed product description that's filled with high-visitors keywords. This will serve to sell customers on the merchandise, as well as boost your store's ranking browsing results. Add your affiliate marketer link to the product posting and share it to your shop.

In your Shopify shop, products could be grouped into categories that help customers navigate your site. Smart collections can immediately group items that meet specific criteria, or you may select which products are grouped together manually. Types of collections are "items under $20," "valentine's time gifts,"Christmas or " goodies." Collections can be used to highlight items that complement one another or cater to a more specific target audience. These collections ought to be presented in the navigation bar of your shop or on the homepage which means that your customers can go to the collection they are interested in without looking through your whole catalog.

Shopify also supplies the opportunity to create a blog page or website for your shop within the platform if you don't already have a single or don't wish to integrate your various other sites. This site offers Google analytics so that you can assess your marketing strategies and monitor how customers are finding your store.

Shopify also offers integrated payment processors like PayPal to help payment processing move more smoothly. When choosing a payment processor, focus on the transaction charges, supported card types, and checkout strategies offered. In the U.S. and U.K., Shopify stores automatically use Shopify Payments which charges a share and a $0.30 flat rate of each transaction in fees to Shopify based upon the subscription bundle the store owner has chosen. Some payment gateways offer off site checkout that redirects a person to the gateway's very own server to total the payment form. Once completed, the client is then directed back to Shopify's confirmation page. Choosing a payment gateway is definitely important to the simple transactions in your store.

When your shop has been built, stocked, and published, you can market it the same manner you would a blog page or a website. Send out email blasts to your email list when your post services or share new content on your own store's blog. Share your store on your own business Facebook page or hyperlink it in the description container of a YouTube product review.

As with other marketing techniques just, do not push your products about the customers. Your function as a reliable influencer is to include value to your customer's life, so when you suggest products it should be to satisfy a need that they have. You may also encourage people inside your network to share posts or links to your web store on their social media. Through the use of your affiliate links in your Shopify shop, you're creating passive income without having to purchase stock or design your own products.

WAY 9: Dropshipping

Dropshipping is a source chain technique that allows an person to earn money by acting while the middleman between a supplier and a customer. The retailer lists products for sale and the customer shall place an order with the ecommerce store. The payment for this item (sold at a markup) can be sent to the accounts of the retailer, and the purchase and shipping information is usually received in the retailer's email. The store then forwards this order and mailing information to the provider and pays the supplier for the merchandise and shipping using the customer's money. The merchandise are ready and shipped directly to the customer. The retailer didn't need to purchase any inventory, spend to store the merchandise, or bother with shipping and delivery out the orders.

If you want to make money with drop-delivery, you'll need the right niche for your shop and the right collection of items to offer. To find a successful niche, consider the best-selling classes on Amazon. When starting out, sell items that are popular in that niche already. Then, as your store's consumer base grows you can include other products. If you don't desire to pick a market, you can run a general store. This allows you to incorporate a number of products and you won't have to worry about being able to incorporate a specific item in to the theme of your store. The benefit of a niche store, however, is that it enables you to build a reputation, or brand, inside your niche which reliability can translate into a far more loyal customer base.

To sell these products, you'll want a website to serve simply because a store. This can be made out of WordPress or a Shopify theme even if you have no coding experience, It is simple to outsource this task to a professional. This store will be your business headquarters, so it must be neat, professional, and easy to navigate. Your website's domain name should be the identical to your store name, therefore take this under consideration when naming your store. The products should be shown with multiple professional searching images and keyword heavy item descriptions.

For a far more cohesive website, it's suggested that you purchase at least one of each product so that you can take original, high quality photos with the same dimensions to share on your site. It is also helpful to own an example of the products because you talk about your experience and testimonials of products on your social media and blogs to operate a vehicle traffic to your shop. You'll also need to choose a payment processor for your site. If you are using Shopify, this is contained in your subscription. Otherwise, you'll have to integrate a payment processor chip into your website.

Shopify also offers apps that allow you to import something to your Shopify shop directly from your supplier's product page without any fuss, along with apps that automate the order fulfillment process. If performed manually, the purchase fulfillment process can get tiresome once your shop starts to grow. When an order comes in, you'll have to visit your suppliers AliExpress store, find the product your customer purchased, and place an order on their behalf. This calls for getting into the client's address, selecting a shipping method, and adding a note to the maker instructing them to avoid placing any invoices or special offers inside the product's packaging. This last step means that your customer doesn't know who your supplier is or how little you paid for the product.

Shopify offers the capability to work with an app that may autofill the address, shipping and delivery information, and the message to your provider when you click to place the purchase on your supplier's site. That is still slightly tedious, but less therefore than manual fulfillment fully. Better options include backend automation systems that handle checkout and item delivery, purchase routing, and shipment tracking. These can be used in combination with various on-line eCommerce platforms and can fully automate the fulfillment aspect of your business. This allows you to be making a passive income once your store is up and operating completely. These backend automation platforms generally have various pricing options based on the amount of orders you need to be fulfilled per month. One example of the plans run at $99 per month for 150 prepared orders. Most others need similar financial investment, although some are cheaper even.

Your store may be prepared to rake in the customers, but you won't have any products to sell if you don't have a supplier. Choosing a trusted supplier is important to the achievement of your business because they will be handling the shipping and delivery of products to customers in your stead. You want a supplier who is efficient and accountable with good customer service. If something goes wrong with the orders, your visitors will contact you and you will be responsible for coping with the supplier, so good customer support is really for your benefit.

It's also ideal to locate a supplier with a warehouse in your nation or near your focus on area so your customers won't obtain stuck waiting months because of their product to ship. You can also reduce this wait period by selecting ePacket when you place the customer's purchase with the supplier. With ePacket, the product should arrive in significantly less than 2 to 3 3 weeks, and you will get a tracking number and that means you know what's occurring with it if your client asks.

Retailers are available on sites want Alibaba or AliExpress. AliExpress runs on the rating system which allows sellers to rate their knowledge with suppliers which makes it easier to narrow down the selection. Once you've narrowed down the potential suppliers, get item samples from each to test the company's focus on detail and customer support. You might be tempted to choose the cheapest supplier so that you can make the largest profit, but the cheapest supplier might possibly not have good quality products or be the best option. Choose the supplier that'll be the very best asset to your store.

To price your items, you can offer them in one of two structures. The first is a normal retail offer where customers pay the full cost listed on your website. This price is, of course, higher than the actual cost of shipping and buying the product. Marking up the product like this lets you make a hefty revenue off of your items, and it leaves room that you can run promotional special discounts while still making a profit. The other pricing framework is a "free plus shipping" offer. This is done by advertising something as cost-free if the customer pays the shipping costs. The "shipping charges" that you charge as a retailer are also marked up, so you're still making a profit. The reason this framework translates well into more sales is that online consumers are already familiar with paying shipping and handling costs with their orders. Whenever an item is presented this actual way, it is easier for them to rationalize the purchase because they are receiving the merchandise itself "free of charge."

You may also gain sales by advertising your store as well as your products in various ways. Find a trustworthy blogger in your market and offer them a free product in trade for a review or recommendation to their audience. This exposure may bring traffic to your store that's primarily made up of individuals in your target audience.

You can even pay to run ads on Facebook and Instagram to market your store. Both of these social media platforms are the greatest for running ads because they're both owned by Facebook which constantly collects data about their users for the precise purpose of running specifically targeted advertisements to them. This means the users subjected to your ads are more likely to actually be part of your market. When you to push out a new product in your shop, you can operate tester ads for some days with a budget of less than $10 per day merely to see how well the product sells. If the merchandise proves itself, you can increase the budget for social media ads.

You can even advertise your store through your own social media platforms and through your email list, and make an effort to get your audience to market your store aswell. Giving your customers an incentive to market your store increase your exposure to your target audience. A discount popup app can be used to advertise a share based discount to customers in exchange for posting your store's website on sociable media, giving their email, or referring a close friend.

Drop-shipping is one of the cheapest methods to open an online business because it doesn't require buying any inventory. You can start a drop-shipping shop for less than $100, but turning that store into a passive income stream shall require investment in outsourcing and automation.

There are some downsides to drop-shipping also. The products you are available are representing you, nevertheless, you don't really get much control over what that representation appears like. Your store does not have any choice over packaging or presentation, even though some suppliers might let you customize these exact things for a fee. Because you will be the face of the product and the retail procedure, you are also held accountable if anything goes incorrect with the merchandise or the shipping. You'll need be the liaison between the customer and the provider, which is one of the reasons it's extremely important to choose the best supplier. You also have to undergo the supplier if you want to contact the shipping company, which can be frustrating and frustrating. Over all, there are dangers involved but drop-shipping can be a great introduction to web business and can provide a buildable source of passive income.

WAY 10: Investing

Investing is among the original, and most intimidating, ways to make passive income. Typically, it takes a substantial financial investment to start producing passive income, but with the rise of technology, it's becoming a lot more practical to invest with as little as $25. Property, stocks, and peer-to-peer lending are three methods for getting started with trading, and it's right now cheaper and simpler to get into than previously.

The most traditional way of investing in property is to buy a rental property with a down payment as high as 20% and lease it out to tenants for a monthly price that covers the mortgage payment and leaves you just a little profit. This purchase requires maintenance and real estate responsibilities or hiring a property manager to take care of the procedures in your stead. This income isn't particularly passive and requires a large initial investment.

Another option for owning a home is to go through a real estate expenditure trust. With these trusts, you spend money on real estate and receive your earnings in dividends. The problem with that is that dividend payments are taxed as normal income, so you don't get the same tax advantages that normal property ownership would provide, including depreciation deduction. By trading with crowdfunding apps, you can find the best of both global worlds. This allows you to really have the tax benefits of property ownership without having to run the house yourself.

FundRise is a real estate crowdfunding site that's growing in popularity. With this web site, you can spend money on real estate with as little as $500. Property companies and designers can propose possibilities to the company's expense team and each proposal undergoes a rigorous screening process. This process ensures that the proposal complies with the strict investment criteria the ongoing company follows. In the final stages of the screening procedure, an investor from FundRise visits the assesses and property it. If the property passes the entire screening process, it really is approved by the expense committee and exposed to investors then.

There are three types of plans these investors can follow. A supplemental income strategy allows the trader to make returns quarterly via dividend obligations. A balanced investment program also allows the investor to get some returns via dividend obligations, but the investor's is allowed by this course of action assets to grow due to asset appreciation. The third program is a long-term growth strategy program. This builds the value of the investor's property through real estate appreciation and escalates the potential for greater value over time. This third plan pays out significantly fewer dividend payments, nonetheless it can be a smart way to develop your assets.

Realty Mogul is another real estate crowdfunding site. This web site requires a minimum investment of $1000, which is certainly twice as much as FundRise, but the annual costs for Realty Mogul are between 0.3% and 0.5% while FundRise has an annual fee of 0.85%.

Another way to get and make passive income is to buy shares of dividend paying out stocks. Many stockbrokers charge around $10 per share trade, but with new apps like Ally Invest trades is often as low as $3.95. If you wish to invest in stocks, research your facts and discover which stocks are the most solid. The even more you invest, the higher the payout you will receive. Dividends are generally paid to your money quarterly, but if you reinvest this dividend you can raise the appreciation of your expense and have larger dividend payouts later on.

With peer-to-peer lending platforms, investors lend cash to borrowers who qualify for traditional loans. The loans are sold off to multiple traders who purchase "notes,fractions or " of the loan. Lending Club is one of the most popular systems for this type of investment. The minimal payment to open an account is $1,000, and this money could be invested across multiple notes. The minimum investment that can be manufactured in one not is certainly $25, and the utmost is $20,000. Many states have a minimum income dependence on $70,000 to qualify as an investor. In some states, this minimum necessity is even higher. However, if your net worth is higher than $250,000 this requirement is waived then.

LendingClub won't allow any investors to invest a lot more than 10% of their net worth in loan notes. If they do invest in a loan, interest is paid on the investment and the debt can be repaid over a span of 36 months or 60 a few months. Returns are between 5% and 9% normally, and they're paid out with little effort with respect to the investor beyond investing the amount of money.

The highest interest rates yield the biggest payouts for investors, but they are connected with borrowers who are bigger credit risks, so investing in these notes might not end well. If the debtor defaults on the mortgage and payment is past due for at least 16 days, the investor must pay a collection fee of 18%. If litigation is involved, the trader has to pay attorney costs and 30% of an attorney's hourly costs. Should the collection attempts fail and the loan reach 150 days past due still, the loan will be charged away and the remaining principal balance of the purchase will be deducted from the traders account. If any money are afterward collected from the borrower, a portion of them will be came back to the investor, but you won't see your cash likely.

Peer-to-peer loans are not insured by the FDIC, which is a risk that is recognized by investors if they get involved with Lending Club. To reduce the likelihood of an instance such as this, you can arranged the requirements when searching for a note so that you are shown debtors with an increased credit score than the 660 minimal Lending Club currently requires, and also paying attention to the loan rankings. Loans are rated based on the borrower's debt to income ratio, the distance of their credit history, their credit scores, and their latest credit activity. Loans have a letter rating between A and G with A getting the highest quality and lowest interest rate and 1 to 5 predicated on the size and length of the mortgage. A small loan with a higher letter grade may be the lowest risk investment.

Investing can be slightly daunting because it is complex and generally requires a larger financial investment. However, it is among the best methods to make real passive income. Once your money is invested, you don't need to do anything to continue attracting profit generally. Bigger investments will yield larger returns generally, but you can start small with these procedures to obtain the lay of the land.

Mentally Approach Online Function

Building a successful business online can enable you to give up your day work and become your own boss. You can obtain started without the financial purchase, and you can marketplace and grow your client-base for free as well. The prospect of growth is unlimited, and you can build a global business that proceeds bringing in money, while you're asleep even. So why isn't everyone getting an online entrepreneur?

The reality about working online is that if you don't have the proper mindset, you won't succeed. Becoming a successful entrepreneur takes a change in perspective from an employee's mindset to a boss's mindset. Employees assume their prospect of income is certainly capped at how much their boss is ready to give them. An employee's mindset will hold you back from recognizing that you will be the only person in charge of how much money you can earn.

No one must give you authorization to earn online, and there is absolutely no limit to how much money you can make if you're ready to learn, grow, and invest enough time and effort. The entrepreneurial mind shall take its destiny into its hands.

A person with a boss's mindset will always be trying to take initiative to develop their business and boost their potential. The successful entrepreneur will compete, self-reliant, and willing to persevere through the struggles of creating a continuing business. Your business might not reach instant success, and at some points, it might involve function that you find tedious or boring. This can lead to a lack of motivation, level of resistance, and procrastination.

The employee-minded individual may lose sight of their vision, decide web business isn't for them, and go back to working their 9 to 5. The business owner will take these difficulties in stride and continue taking steps toward their objective to persevere through tough times. These defining occasions differentiate between a successful business and a failed desire. For the most effective entrepreneurs, failure is simply not an option. A pessimistic view will sabotage your business before it begins actually. Through dedication, determination, and relentless function you can perform boundless success, in the online market especially.

One of the best ways to ensure you strategy your online business with the proper mindset right from the start is to draw up a business plan. Yes, business plans are often created for presenting to investors, which you're not likely doing with this on the web startup, but outlining the facts of your business in writing will give you an improved vision for what you're operating toward. Having this eyesight will help you persevere when you begin to lose motivation. You should also be directly involved with as many areas of your business as possible during the beginning of its development.

Research your facts and ensure you're alert to what's going on, that way you could have a better knowledge of how the process works and you will better optimize your functions moving forward. Learn as much as you can about your business before you begin, and continue to find out as you go. These two steps will help you in the grand scheme with understanding the big picture and learning how to achieve it. Nevertheless, on a day-to-time basis, working for yourself in an web business can be harder than you expect, despite having a clear vision.

When you're able to work whenever and wherever you want, it could almost become too much freedom. Your work hours are versatile, so that you can sleep past due and choose to indulge in other things during occasions when you'd normally become working, but no-one can otherwise tell you. If you want to succeed, it's important to remember that your online business is still a business, and it needs to be operate as such. To keep the most optimal productivity as an ongoing business, you will need to optimize your efficiency as an individual.

To do therefore, you need to build the healthy practices, both physical and mental, that will lead you toward achievement. Carrying out a sleep schedule that allows you sufficient relax every full night will help to avoid drowsiness and mind fog. Incorporating exercise and a healthy diet will improve energy and mental clarity, and also reducing the effects of stress in your thoughts and body. These simple habits will help you maintain your physical health, as well as assisting to improve your mental clarity and health.

It's also advisable to regularly set aside time to enjoy personal development in order to continually be bettering yourself and maintaining your drive. Develop your teamwork and task management skills, and also leadership, communication, and romantic relationship building. Practice and meditate maintaining a positive and motivated attitude. Concentrating on these aspects will help you discover ways to approach the difficulties of an entrepreneurial lifestyle in an effective way.

Furthermore to these personal habits, you should establish solid work habits also. Set aside specific times to focus on your business without distractions. Make lists of big picture goals for your business, then break that list into monthly goals. The monthly goals could be divided further into weekly goals even, those weekly goals should be broken down into daily tasks and goals. Order daily these job lists 1st by time-sensitivity, by ROI then. ROI refers to "return on investment." Tasks that may yield a larger benefit in comparison to the effort you put in ought to be completed before jobs that will take an purchase of commitment but not yield as important a benefit. Prize yourself for accomplishing an objective, and then turn your focus directly to what's next.

Make sure to schedule particular time blocks dedicated to working, and keep this right time as split as possible from your own time with family and friends. Preserving this separation of worlds can give you time from your business which is essential to your mental wellness. Surround yourself with positive, dedicated, and motivational individuals who enable you to stay centered on your goals. Particularly if your business is run out of your home, be sure to maintain as much separation as you can between your work space and your personal space. This enables you to keep a business-minded view of your work time, along with preventing any potential stress on your personal life during the higher-stress entrance loading period of your business.

Essentially, in order to succeed simply because an online entrepreneur working toward passive income, you have to stay positive, dedicated, and focused on your goal. Look after yourself and mentally physically, build healthy habits, and continually be growing as an individual and as a businessperson. The more you learn and develop, the better an asset you are to yourself as well as your entrepreneurial dreams.

Conclusion

Thank for making it through to the finish of this guide, let's hope it had been informative and able to provide you with all the tools you need to reach your passive income goals!

There are no limitations on how much cash you can generate online if you are ready to invest the time and work into growing your business. You don't even need a financial purchase to get started, so what's keeping you back?

One of the best places to begin is to start out a blog and begin sharing articles to build your online presence. Having a blog will help in nearly any method of earning passive income since it serves as a central hub where one can promote your ventures. It takes time to begin building passive income, but it is never as well late to start.

Made in the USA
Middletown, DE
14 June 2019